URBAN
TRAILS
EVERETT

URBAN TRAILS

TRAILS
EVERETT

Western Snohomish County
Whidbey Island · Camano Island

CRAIG ROMANO

MOUNTAINEERS
BOOKS

MOUNTAINEERS BOOKS is the publishing division of The Mountaineers, an organization founded in 1906 and dedicated to the exploration, preservation, and enjoyment of outdoor and wilderness areas.

1001 SW Klickitat Way, Suite 201, Seattle, WA 98134
800.553.4453, www.mountaineersbooks.org

Printed in China
Distributed in the United Kingdom by Cordee, www.cordee.co.uk
First edition, 2019

Copyeditor: Sarah Gorecki, Outdoor Prose
Design: Jen Grable
Layout: McKenzie Long, Cardinal Innovative
Cartographer: Pease Press Cartography

Cover photograph: *Filtered sunlight at Trillium Community Forest (Trail 28)*
Frontispiece: *View south of Admiralty Inlet from the Bluff Trail in Ebey's Landing (Trail 32)*

Library of Congress Cataloging-in-Publication Data
Names: Romano, Craig author.
Title: Urban trails. Everett : Western Snohomish County, Camano Island, Whidbey Island / Craig Romano.
Other titles: Everett
Description: First edition. | Seattle, Washington : Mountaineers Books, [2019] | Includes index.
Identifiers: LCCN 2018005753 (print) | LCCN 2018012741 (ebook) | ISBN 9781680510317 (Ebook) | ISBN 9781680510300 (paperback)
Subjects: LCSH: Hiking—Washington (State)—Everett—Guidebooks. | Walking—Washington (State)—Everett—Guidebooks. | Running—Washington (State)—Everett—Guidebooks. | Trails—Washington (State)—Everett—Guidebooks. | Outdoor recreation—Washington (State)—Everett—Guidebooks. | Hiking—Washington (State)—Island County—Guidebooks. | Walking—Washington (State)—Island County—Guidebooks. | Running—Washington (State)—Island County—Guidebooks. | Trails—Washington (State)—Island County—Guidebooks. | Outdoor recreation—Washington (State)—Island County—Guidebooks. | Everett (Wash.)—Guidebooks. | Island County (Wash.)—Guidebooks.
Classification: LCC GV199.42.W2 (ebook) | LCC GV199.42.W2 R675 2019 (print) | DDC 796.5109797/75—dc23
LC record available at https://lccn.loc.gov/2018005753

Mountaineers Books titles may be purchased for corporate, educational, or other promotional sales, and our authors are available for a wide range of events. For information on special discounts or booking an author, contact our customer service at 800-553-4453 or mbooks@mountaineersbooks.org.

Printed on FSC® certified materials
ISBN (paperback): 978-1-68051-030-0
ISBN (ebook): 978-1-68051-031-7

MIX
Paper from responsible sources
FSC® C008047
www.fsc.org

CONTENTS

WHIDBEY ISLAND

CAMANO ISLAND

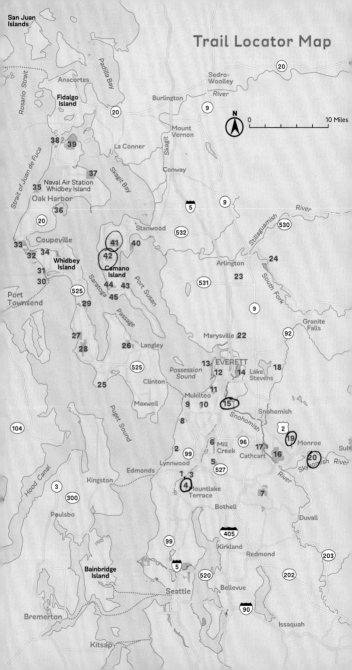

TRAILS AT A GLANCE

Trail and/or Park	Distance	Walk	Hike	Run	Kids	Dogs
EVERETT AND WESTERN SNOHOMISH COUNTY						
1. Scriber Lake	1.2 miles of trails	•			•	•
2. Meadowdale Beach Park	2.5 miles roundtrip		•	•	•	•
3. Interurban Trail	up to 11.4 miles roundtrip	•		•	•	•
4. Terrace Creek Park	2 miles roundtrip	•	*3/16/19.*		•	•
5. North Creek Park	2 miles roundtrip	•	•		•	•
6. North Creek Trail	4.8 miles roundtrip	•		•	•	•
7. Paradise Valley Conservation Area	13 miles of trails		•	•	•	•
8. Big Gulch	2.7 miles of trails		•	•		•
9. Japanese Gulch Conservation Area	more than 7 miles of trails		•	•	•	•
10. Narbeck Wetland Sanctuary	1.8 miles of trails	•	•		•	part
11. Forest Park	1.5 miles of trails	•		•	•	•
12. Everett Waterfront Trail	6 miles of trails	•		•	•	•
13. Jetty Island	more than 2 miles of beach	•			•	
14. Langus Riverfront Park and Spencer Island	more than 5 miles of trails	•	•	•	•	part
15. Lowell Riverfront Park	4 miles roundtrip	•	*yes*	•	•	•
16. Lord Hill Regional Park	more than 30 miles of trails		•	•	•	•
17. Bob Heirman Wildlife Preserve at Thomas Eddy	1.5 miles roundtrip		•		•	

Trail and/or Park	Distance	Walk	Hike	Run	Kids	Dogs
18. Centennial Trail	29.5 miles one-way	•		•	•	•
19. Lake Tye Park	1.6 miles roundtrip	•		•	•	•
20. Al Borlin Park	about 1.5 miles of trails	•		•	•	•
21. Osprey Park	2 miles of trails	•		•	•	•
22. Jennings Memorial Park	1.5 miles of trails	•		•	•	•
23. Arlington Airport Trail	5.5 miles roundtrip	•		•	•	•
24. River Meadows Park	6 miles of trails		•	•	•	•
WHIDBEY ISLAND						
25. Double Bluff	4 miles roundtrip	•	•		•	•
26. Saratoga Woods, Putney Woods, and Metcalf Trust Trails	more than 15 miles of trails	•	•	•	•	•
27. South Whidbey State Park	4 miles of trails		•		•	•
28. Trillium Community Forest	7 miles of trails		•	•	•	•
29. Greenbank Farm	more than 4 miles of trails	•	•	•	•	•
30. Fort Casey Historical State Park	1.8 miles of trails/ more than 2 miles of beach	•	•		•	•
31. Admiralty Inlet Preserve	2.3 miles of trails	•	•			•
32. Ebey's Landing National Historical Reserve	5.2 miles		•		•	•
33. Fort Ebey State Park	more than 30 miles of trails	•	•	•	•	•
34. Kettles Trail	3.6 miles one-way	•			•	•

(handwritten annotations next to rows 19 and 20: "many times", "3·17 2019")

Trail and/or Park	Distance	Walk	Hike	Run	Kids	Dogs
35. Joseph Whidbey State Park	2 miles of trails	•	•		•	•
36. Oak Harbor Waterfront Trails	more than 3 miles of trails	•		•	•	•
37. Dugualla State Park	more than 5 miles of trails		•	•	•	•
38. Deception Pass State Park: Goose Rock and Cranberry Lake	more than 7 miles of trails	•	•	•	•	•
39. Deception Pass State Park: Hoypus Point Natural Forest Area	more than 9 miles of trails	•	•	•	•	•
CAMANO ISLAND						
40. Iverson Spit Preserve 3·10·19	1.2 miles of trails	•	•		•	•
41. Camano Ridge Forest Preserve can't find TH 10.27.19	more than 5 miles of trails					
42. Four Springs Lake Preserve Found TH 10.27.19	1.5 miles of trails			•	•	•
43. Elger Bay Preserve	2.5 miles of trails		•	•	•	•
44. Cama Beach Historical State Park	more than 5 miles of trails	•	•	•	•	•
45. Camano Island State Park	more than 4 miles of trails	•	•	•	•	•

INTRODUCTION

TRAILS FOR FUN AND FITNESS IN YOUR BIG BACKYARD

LET'S FACE IT: WHETHER YOU'RE a hiker, walker, or runner, life can get in the way when it comes to putting time in on the trail. Far too often, it's hard for most of us to set aside an hour—never mind a day, or even longer—to hit the trails of our favorite parks and forests strewn across the state. But that doesn't mean we can't get out on the trail more frequently. Right in and near our own communities are thousands of acres of parks and nature preserves containing hundreds of miles of trails. And we can visit these pocket wildernesses, urban and urban-fringe parks and preserves, greenbelts, and trail corridors on a whim—for an hour or two without having to drive far. Some of these places we can even visit without driving at all—hopping on the bus instead—lessening our carbon footprint while giving us more time to relax from our hurried schedules.

Urban Trails: Everett focuses on the myriad of trails, parks, and preserves within the urban, suburban, and rural-fringe areas in Everett, Western Snohomish County, Camano Island, and Whidbey Island. You'll find trails to beaches, old-growth

Opposite: *Everett's Forest Park living up to its name (Trail 11)*

13

Author running on the Centennial Trail near the Nakashima Barn (Trail 18)

forests, lakeshores, riverfronts, shorelines, wildlife-rich wet-lands, rolling hills, scenic vistas, meadows, historic sites, and vibrant neighborhoods and communities. While often we equate hiking trails with the state's wildernesses and forests, there are plenty of areas of natural beauty and accessi-ble trails in the midst of our population centers. The routes included here are designed to show you where you can go for a good run, long walk, or quick hike right in your own backyard.

This guide has two missions. One is to promote fitness and get you outside more often! A trip to Mount Rainier, North Cascades, or Olympic national parks can be a major under-taking for many of us. But a quick outdoor getaway to a local park or trail can be done almost anytime—before work, during a lunch break, after work, or when we don't feel like fighting traffic and driving for miles. And all of these trails are available year-round, so you can walk, run, or hike every day by utilizing the trails within your own neighborhood. If you feel you are not getting outside enough or getting enough exercise, this book can help you achieve a healthier lifestyle.

Mission number two of this guide is to promote the local parks, preserves, and trails that exist within and near our urban areas. More than 4.7 million people (65 percent of the state's population) call the greater Puget Sound home. While conservationists continue to promote protection of our state's large, roadless wild corners—and that is still important—it's equally important that we promote the preservation of natural areas and develop more trails and greenbelts right where people live. Why? For one thing, the Puget Sound area contains unique and threatened ecosystems that deserve to be protected as much as our wilder remote places. And, we need to have usable and accessible trails where people live, work, and spend the majority of their time.

Urban trails and parks allow folks to bond with nature and be outside on a regular basis. They help us cut our carbon footprint by giving us access to recreation without burning excessive gallons of fuel to reach a destination. They make it easier for us to commit to regular exercise programs, giving us safe and agreeable places to walk, run, and hike. And urban trails and parks also allow for disadvantaged populations—folks who may not have cars or the means to travel to one of our national parks or forests—a chance to experience nature and a healthy lifestyle too. As the greater Puget Sound area continues to grow in population and becomes increasingly more crowded and developed, it is all the more important that we support the expansion of our urban parks and trails. So get out there, get fit, and have fun! And don't forget to advocate for more trails and parks.

HOW TO USE THIS GUIDE

THIS EASY-TO-USE GUIDE PROVIDES YOU with enough details to get out on the trail with confidence, while leaving enough room for your own personal discovery. I have walked, hiked, or run every mile of the trails described here, and the directions and advice are accurate and up to date. Conditions can and do change, however, so make sure you check on the status of a park or trail before you go.

THE DESTINATIONS

This book includes forty-five destinations, covering trails in and around Everett, Arlington, Lynnwood, Marysville, Mill Creek, Monroe, Mukilteo, Snohomish, Sultan, and Camano and Whidbey islands. Each one begins with the park or trail name. Next is a block of information detailing the following:

Distance. Here you will find roundtrip mileage (unless otherwise noted) if the route describes a single trail or the total mileage of trails within the park, preserve, or greenway if the route gives an overview of the destination's trail system. Note that while I have measured most of the trails in this book with GPS and have consulted maps and governing land agencies, the distance stated may not always be exact—but it'll be pretty darn close.

Elevation gain. For individual trails, elevation gain is for the *cumulative* difference on the route (and return), meaning not only the difference between the high and low points on the trail, but also for all other significant changes in elevation along the way. For destinations where multiple routes are given, as in a trail network within a park, the elevation gain applies to the steepest trail on the route.

High point. The high point is the highest elevation of the trail or trail system described. Almost all of the trails in the book are at a relatively low elevation, ensuring mostly snow-free winter access.

Difficulty. This factor is based not only on length and elevation gain of a trail or trails but also on the type of tread and surface area of the trail(s). Most of the trails in this book are easy or moderate for the average hiker, walker, or runner. Depending on your level of fitness, you may find the trails more or less difficult than described.

Fitness. This description denotes whether the trail is best for hikers, walkers, or runners. Generally, paved trails will be of more interest to walkers and runners, while rough, hilly trails will appeal more to hikers. Of course you are free to hike, walk, or run (unless running is specifically prohibited) on any of the trails in this book.

Family-friendly. Here you'll find notes on a trail's or park's suitability for children and any cautions to be aware of, such as cliffs, heavy mountain-bike use, and so on. Some trails may be noted as ADA-accessible and suitable for jogging strollers.

Dog-friendly. This denotes whether dogs are allowed on the trail and what regulations (such as leashed and under control) apply.

Amenities. The featured park's amenities can include privies, drinking water, benches, interpretive signs or displays, shelters, learning centers, and campgrounds, to name a few.

Contact/maps. Here you'll find contact info for the trail's or park's managing agency and where to get current trail

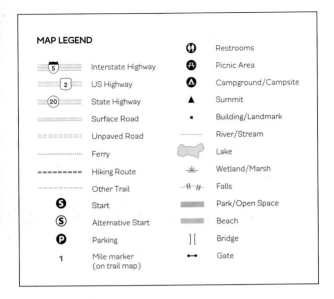

MAP LEGEND

5	Interstate Highway
2	US Highway
20	State Highway
	Surface Road
	Unpaved Road
	Ferry
	Hiking Route
	Other Trail
S	Start
⑤	Alternative Start
P	Parking
1	Mile marker (on trail map)

🚻	Restrooms
🍴	Picnic Area
▲	Campground/Campsite
▲	Summit
▪	Building/Landmark
	River/Stream
	Lake
	Wetland/Marsh
	Falls
	Park/Open Space
	Beach
] [	Bridge
•—•	Gate

conditions. All websites and phone numbers for trail and park managers or governing agencies can be found in the Resources section at the back of the book. These websites will often direct you to trail and park maps; in some cases, a better or supplemental map (such as Green Trails) is noted.

GPS. GPS coordinates in degrees and decimal minutes (based on the WGS84 datum) are provided for the main trailhead, to help get you to the trail.

Before you go. This section notes any fees or permits required, hours the park or preserve is open (if limited), closures, and any other special concerns.

Next, I describe how to get to the trailhead via your own vehicle or by public transit if available.

Double Bluff beach (Trail 25)

GETTING THERE. Driving: Provides directions to the trailhead—generally from the nearest freeway exit, major road, and in the case of Whidbey Island, ferry terminal. Often I state directions from more than one destination—and I provide parking information. **Transit:** If the trailhead is served by public transportation, this identifies the bus agency and line.

EACH HIKE begins with an overview of the featured park or trail, highlighting its setting and character, with notes on the property's conservation history.

GET MOVING. This section describes the route or trails and what you might find on your hike, walk, or run, and may note additional highlights beyond the trail itself, such as points of historical interest.

GO FARTHER. Here you'll find suggestions for making your hike, walk, or run longer within the featured park—or perhaps by combining this trip with an adjacent park or trail.

PERMITS, REGULATIONS, AND PARK FEES

Many of the trails and parks described in this book are managed by county and city parks departments, requiring no permits or fees. Destinations managed by Washington State Parks and the Washington Department of Natural Resources (DNR) require a day-use fee in the form of the Discover Pass (www.discoverpass.wa.gov) for vehicle access. A Discover Pass can be purchased per vehicle per day or annually for up to two vehicles. You can purchase the pass online, at many retail outlets, or better yet, from a state park office to avoid the handling fee. Each hike in this book clearly states if a fee is charged or a pass is required.

Regulations such as whether dogs are allowed or a park has restricted hours or is closed for certain occasions (such as during high fire danger or for wildlife management) are clearly spelled out in each trail's information block.

ROAD AND TRAIL CONDITIONS

In general, trails change little year to year. But change can occur, and sometimes very quickly. A heavy storm can wash out sections of trail or access road in moments. Wind storms can blow down multiple trees across trails, making paths impassable. Lack of adequate funding is also responsible for trail neglect and degradation. For some of the wilder destinations in this book it is wise to contact the appropriate land manager after a significant weather event to check on current trail and road conditions.

On the topic of trail conditions, it is vital that we acknowledge the thousands of volunteers who donate tens of thousands of hours to trail maintenance each year. The Washington Trails Association (WTA) alone coordinates more than 150,000 hours of volunteer trail maintenance each year. But there is always a need for more. Our trail system faces ever-increasing threats, including lack of adequate trail funding. Consider

Al Emerson Nature Trail in Camano Island State Park (Trail 45)

joining one or more of the trail and conservation groups listed in the Resources section at the end of the book.

OUTDOOR ETHICS

Strong, positive outdoor ethics include making sure you leave the trail (and park) in as good a condition as you found it—or even better. Get involved with groups and organizations that safeguard, watchdog, and advocate for land protection. And get on the phone and keyboard, and let land managers and public officials know how important protecting lands and trails is to you.

All of us who recreate in Washington's natural areas have a moral obligation and responsibility to respect and protect our natural heritage. Everything we do on the planet has an impact—and we should strive to have as little negative impact as possible. The Leave No Trace Center for Outdoor Ethics is

Temple Pond Trail in Lords Hill Regional Park (Trail 16)

an educational, nonpartisan, nonprofit organization that was developed for responsible enjoyment and active stewardship of the outdoors. Their program helps educate outdoor enthusiasts about their recreational impacts and recommends techniques to prevent and minimize such impacts. While geared toward backcountry use, many Leave No Trace (LNT) principles are also sound advice for urban and urban-fringe parks too, including planning ahead, disposing of waste properly, and being considerate of other visitors. Visit www.lnt.org to learn more.

TRAIL ETIQUETTE

We need to be sensitive not only to the environment surrounding our trails but to other trail users as well. Some of the trails in this book are also open to mountain bikers and equestrians. When you encounter other trail users, whether they are hikers, runners, bicyclists, or horseback riders, the only hard-and-fast rule is to follow common sense and exercise simple courtesy. With this Golden Rule of Trail Etiquette firmly in mind, here are other things you can do during trail encounters to make everyone's trip more enjoyable:

- **Observe the right-of-way.** When meeting bicyclists or horseback riders, those of us on foot should move off the trail. This is because hikers, walkers, and runners are more mobile and flexible than other users, making it easier for us to quickly step off the trail.
- **Move aside for horses.** When meeting horseback riders specifically, step off the downhill side of the trail unless the terrain makes this difficult or dangerous. In that case, move to the uphill side of the trail, but crouch down a bit so you do not tower over the horses' heads. Also, make yourself visible so as not to spook the big beastie, and talk in a normal voice to the riders. This calms the horses. If walking with a dog, keep your buddy under control.

Deception Pass Bridge from North Beach (Trail 38)

- **Stay on trails.** Don't cut switchbacks, take shortcuts, or make new trails; all lead to erosion and unsightly trail degradation.
- **Obey the rules specific to the trail or park you are visiting.** Many trails are closed to certain types of use, including dogs and mountain bikes. Some trails are bike only—don't walk on them.
- **Keep dogs under control.** Trail users who bring dogs should have their dog on a leash or under very strict voice-command at all times. And if leashes are required, then this does apply to you. Many trail users who have had negative encounters with dogs (actually

with the dog owners) on the trail are not fond of, or are even afraid of, encountering dogs. Respect their right not to be approached by your darling pooch. A well-behaved, leashed dog, however, can certainly help warm up these folks to a canine encounter. And always pack out your dog's poop and dispose of it properly.

- **Avoid disturbing wildlife.** Observe from a distance, resisting the urge to move closer to wildlife (use your telephoto lens). This not only keeps you safer but also prevents the animal from having to exert itself unnecessarily to flee from you.
- **Take only photographs.** Leave all natural features and historic artifacts as you found them for others to enjoy.
- **Never roll rocks off trails or cliffs.** Gravity increases the impact of falling rocks exponentially, and you risk endangering lives below you.
- **Mind the music.** Not everyone (almost no one) wants to hear your blaring music. If you like listening to music while you run, hike, or walk, wear headphones and respect other trail users' right to peace and quiet—and to listening to nature's music.

HUNTING
Nearly all of the destinations in this book are closed to hunting. However, a couple of areas are open to game and bird hunting and are noted. While using trails in areas frequented by hunters, it is best to make yourself visible by donning an orange cap and vest. If hiking with a dog, your buddy should wear an orange vest too.

BEARS AND COUGARS
While the chance of spotting a bear in the Everett area is pretty rare, Washington harbors healthy populations of black

bears in many of the parks and preserves along the urban fringe. If you encounter a bear while hiking, you'll usually just catch a glimpse of its bear behind. But occasionally the bruin may actually want to get a look at *you*.

To avoid an un-*bear*-able encounter, practice bear-aware prudence: Always keep a safe distance. Remain calm, do not look a bear in the eyes, speak in a low tone, and do not run from it. Hold your arms out to appear as big as possible. Slowly move away. The bear may bluff charge—do not run. If he does attack, fight back using fists, rocks, trekking poles, or bear spray if you are carrying it.

Washington supports a healthy population of *Felix concolor*. While cougar encounters are extremely rare, they do occur—even occasionally on the urban fringe. In 2018 a bicyclist was killed by a cougar outside of North Bend. Cougars are cats—they're curious. They may follow hikers, but rarely (almost never) attack humans. Minimize contact by not hiking or running alone and by avoiding carrion. If you do encounter a cougar, remember it's looking for prey that can't or won't fight back. Don't run. This may trigger its prey instinct. Stand and face it. If you appear aggressive, the cougar will probably back down. Wave your arms, trekking poles, or a jacket over your head to appear bigger, and maintain eye contact. Pick up children and small dogs and back away slowly if you can do so safely, not taking your eyes off of it. If it attacks, throw things at it. Shout loudly. If it gets close, whack it with your trekking pole, fighting back aggressively.

WATER AND GEAR

While most of the trails in this book can be enjoyed without much preparation or gear, it is always a good idea to bring water, even if you're just out for a quick walk or run. Even better, carry a small pack with water, a few snacks, sunglasses, and a rain jacket.

THE TEN ESSENTIALS

If you are heading out for a longer adventure—perhaps an all-day hike in one of Whidbey Island's large parks—consider packing the **Ten Essentials**, a list (developed by The Mountaineers) of items that are good to have on hand in an emergency:

1. **Navigation.** Carry a map of the area you plan to be in and know how to read it. A cell phone or GPS unit are good to have along too.
2. **Headlamp.** If caught out after dark, you'll be glad you have a headlamp or flashlight so you can follow the trail home.
3. **Sun protection.** Even on wet days, carry sunscreen and sunglasses; you never know when the clouds will lift, and you can easily sunburn near water.
4. **First aid.** At the very least, your kit should include bandages, gauze, scissors, tape, tweezers, pain relievers, antiseptics, and perhaps a small manual.
5. **Knife.** A pocketknife or multitool can come in handy, as can basic repair items such as nylon cord, safety pins, a small roll of duct tape, and a small tube of superglue.
6. **Fire.** While being forced to spend the night out is not likely on these trails, a campfire could provide welcome warmth in an emergency, with matches kept dry in a zip-lock bag.
7. **Shelter.** This can be as simple as a garbage bag or a rain poncho that can double as an emergency tarp.
8. **Extra food.** Pack a handful of nuts or sports bars for emergency pick-me-ups.
9. **Extra water.** Bring enough water to keep you hydrated, and for longer treks consider a means of water purification.
10. **Extra clothes.** Storms can and do blow in rapidly. Carry raingear, wind gear, and extra layers.

SAFETY CONCERNS

By and large, our parks and trails are safe places. Common sense and vigilance, however, are still in order. This is true for all trail users, but particularly so for solo ones. Be aware of your surroundings at all times. Let someone know when and where you're headed out.

Sadly, car break-ins are a common occurrence at some of our parks and trailheads. Absolutely under no circumstances leave anything of value in your vehicle while out on the trail. Take your wallet and smartphone with you. A duffel bag on the back seat may contain dirty T-shirts, but a thief may think there's a laptop in it. Save yourself the hassle of returning to a busted window by not giving criminals a reason to clout your car.

Vagrants and substance abuse are concerns at several of our urban parks as well. It's best not to wander off trail, and if you come upon a homeless encampment, leave the area

Trail marker at Trillium Woods (Trail 28)

and report the situation to the authorities. Be aware of nee-
dles, human waste, and other hazardous debris around such
encampments. Parks and trails where this is a serious concern
have been omitted from this book.

No need to be paranoid, though, for our trails and parks
are fairly safe places. Just use a little common sense and vigilance while you're out and about.

A NOTE ABOUT SAFETY

Safety is an important concern in all outdoor activities. No guidebook
can alert you to every hazard or anticipate the limitations of every
reader. Therefore, the descriptions of roads, trails, routes, and natural
features in this book are not representations that a particular place or
excursion will be safe for your party. When you follow any of the routes
described in this book, you assume responsibility for your own safety.
Under normal conditions, such excursions require the usual attention
to traffic, road and trail conditions, weather, terrain, the capabilities of
your party, and other factors. Some of the lands in this book are subject
to development or change of ownership. Always check current conditions and obey posted private property signs. Keeping informed on
current conditions and exercising common sense are the keys to a safe,
enjoyable outing.

—*Mountaineers Books*

Next page: *Temple Pond (Trail 16)*

EVERETT AND WESTERN SNOHOMISH COUNTY

Now synonymous with Boeing, the navy, and a thriving aerospace economy, Everett was once a gritty city of mills and smokestacks. Snohomish County seat and now home to over 110,000 residents, Everett is Washington's seventh-largest city and a major employment center in the Puget Sound region. While the city has changed much since its resources-dependent past, it still retains vestiges of its early days, including some charming old neighborhoods and historic buildings. And the city has never looked better, especially its waterfront, which is currently being redeveloped with parks, trails, shops, restaurants, and residences.

Everett and Snohomish County have experienced explosive growth over the past few decades. Fueled in part by neighboring Seattle's growth and lack of affordable housing, Snohomish County is now the third most populated county in the state, with more than 800,000 residents. Unfortunately the county hasn't kept pace with expanding its parks and trails to accommodate its burgeoning population. Still, the parks and trails that grace the county provide excellent hiking, walking, and running opportunities—and almost always with views of surrounding mountains and waterways. And a handful of vestiges of the county's industrial and agricultural past remain preserved within these parks among all of the new suburban housing developments.

1   Scriber Lake

DISTANCE:	1.2 miles of trails
ELEVATION GAIN:	Minimal
HIGH POINT:	335 feet
DIFFICULTY:	Easy
FITNESS:	Walkers
FAMILY-FRIENDLY:	Yes, and jogging stroller and wheelchair accessible
DOG-FRIENDLY:	On leash
AMENITIES:	Restrooms, picnic tables, interpretive signs, benches, water
CONTACT/MAPS:	Lynnwood Parks and Recreation; map not available online
GPS:	N 47˚ 49.191', W 122˚ 18.528'
BEFORE YOU GO:	Park open dawn to dusk.

GETTING THERE

Driving from Everett: Take I-5 to exit 181 and follow State Route 524 (196th Street SW) west 1.4 miles, turning left onto Scriber Lake Road. After 0.1 mile turn left onto 198th Street SW and continue 0.1 mile to the trailhead at Scriber Lake Park on your left.

Driving from Seattle: Take I-5 to exit 181A. Turn left onto 44th Avenue NW and proceed 0.2 mile. Then turn left onto 200th Street SW and drive 0.8 mile. Next turn right onto 56th Avenue W (road becomes 198th Street SW) and drive 0.1 mile to the trailhead at Scriber Lake Park on your right.

Transit: Community Transit Route 196 (Routes 116, 120 service Scriber Creek Trail on 200th Street SW.)

Who would imagine that lying right in the center of Lynnwood's sea of stores, restaurants, and commercial developments is a wildlife-rich wetland complex of pond, peat bog, and streams? Wedged between bustling boulevards is little Scriber Lake Park, a surprisingly delightful natural area graced

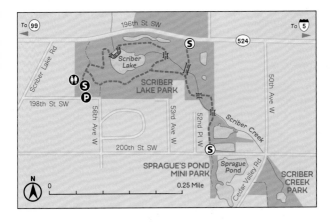

with good trails, interpretive signage, and wildlife-themed, wrought-iron park benches. Perfect for late afternoon strolls and early morning jaunts, Scriber Lake is also an ideal destination for inquisitive children.

GET MOVING

From the trailhead, follow a wide, soft-surfaced trail to a junction. You can go either way to loop around the small lake. Start your explorations. Scan the shoreline and its swampy surrounding thickets of shrubbery for a myriad of wading and nesting birds, scurrying small mammals, and insect-craving amphibians. You'll definitely want to linger long on the floating boardwalk that protrudes into Scriber Lake. Here you can be entertained by whimsical waterfowl and admire a small corner of Lynnwood that has virtually remained the same since the time Paul Schreiber homesteaded it in the 1890s.

While the hike around the lake is short, a few spurs lead from it and you can follow a paved path along Scriber Creek to add distance. A side trail diverts off of this trail to cross the creek and traverse a wetland forest—terminating on busy 196th Street SW. The Scriber Creek Trail skirts some homes

Happy hikers on Scriber Lake's floating dock

and apartments, coming to 200th Street SW. Carefully cross the road and walk a little more in Sprague's Pond Mini Park. Here kids will want to take to the playground or watch the resident waterfowl. Return to your start after a satisfying visit.

GO FARTHER

Walk a short distance on sidewalks along 200th Street SW and Cedar Valley Road to Scriber Creek Park. From there you can follow the Scriber Creek Trail for 0.25 mile to the Lynnwood Transit Center (for bus access) and connect with the Interurban Trail (see Trail 3).

2 Meadowdale Beach Park

DISTANCE:	2.5 miles roundtrip
ELEVATION GAIN:	425 feet
HIGH POINT:	425 feet
DIFFICULTY:	Moderate
FITNESS:	Hikers, runners
FAMILY-FRIENDLY:	Yes
DOG-FRIENDLY:	On leash
AMENITIES:	Restrooms, picnic tables, interpretive signs, benches
CONTACT/MAPS:	Snohomish County Parks
GPS:	N 47° 51.428', W 122° 18.946'
BEFORE YOU GO:	Park open 7:00 AM to dusk; do not park on road.

GETTING THERE

Driving: From Everett or Seattle take I-5 to exit 183. Then follow 164th Street SW west for 1.5 miles, bearing left onto 44th Avenue W. Continue for 0.4 mile and turn right onto 168th Street SW. Now drive west (passing State Route 99) for 0.5 mile and turn right onto 52nd Avenue W. In another 0.5 mile turn left onto 160th Street SW (signed for Meadowdale County Park). Drive 0.2 mile and turn right onto 56th Avenue W. Continue

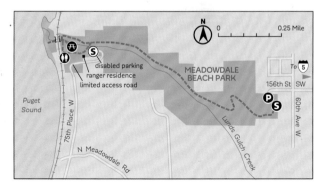

0.3 mile and turn left onto 156th Street SW, following this road a short distance to the park entrance and trailhead.

Hike through a deep, green ravine cradling a salmon-spawning stream to a quiet Puget Sound beach granting sweeping views of Whidbey Island and the Olympic Mountains. Meadowdale Beach Park's Lunds Gulch forms a green swath in heavily sub-urbanized south Snohomish County. The 108-acre park is not only a coveted recreation area for residents but also a refuge for area wildlife.

GET MOVING

The trail through Lunds Gulch (along Lunds Gulch Creek) begins in a small grassy opening on a forested bluff. The wide and well-built trail immediately enters a mature forest of Douglas fir and wastes no time dropping more than 400 feet into the emerald ravine. Sturdy steps constructed by the Washington Trails Association help you negotiate the descent.

Big boughs of ferns line the way, as do hefty cedar and hemlock stumps, testaments to the giants that once flour-ished here before pioneering loggers "discovered" them. Not all of the big trees here were harvested, though: a few giant firs, cottonwoods, and Sitka spruce still stand tall within the lush gulch. John Lund first homesteaded this rugged tract back in 1878, and today it is nicely reverting back to its wilder days. The trail crosses some side creeks, eventually coming alongside the small creek named after Lund. The waterway makes a short journey to the Sound—but it's an important run, supporting spawning salmon; visit in the fall to see them.

In 1 mile the trail comes to a junction. The path left leads to the ranger's residence and to picnic tables scattered about on a manicured lawn. You'll find a restroom here, too. Much of this area once sported a country club complete with an Olympic-sized swimming pool and bath houses. In 1968 the

Forested Lunds Gulch

county parks department acquired this property and began transforming it into a top-notch natural and recreational gem.

Continue hiking straight along the creek and through forest, eventually coming to a railroad underpass. Now make tracks under the tracks to reach the beach. When the tide is low you can roam for some distance on extensive flats. Rest on a driftwood log, comb the shore, and enjoy a splendid view of Whidbey Island and the Olympic Mountains. Sunsets are supreme here, but don't forget to allot yourself some daylight for the return to your vehicle.

GO FARTHER

In nearby Edmonds, you can check out two small but delightful natural areas for short hikes. Yost Park and Southwest County Park both contain a little more than a mile of trails—and they are both far less traveled than Meadowdale Beach Park.

---

3   Interurban Trail

DISTANCE:	Up to 11.4 miles roundtrip
ELEVATION GAIN:	Up to 250 feet
HIGH POINT:	425 feet
DIFFICULTY:	Easy
FITNESS:	Walkers, runners
FAMILY-FRIENDLY:	Yes, south of Lynnwood Transit Center
DOG-FRIENDLY:	On leash
AMENITIES:	Restrooms, picnic tables, benches at adjacent parks
CONTACT/MAPS:	Snohomish County Parks
GPS:	N 47° 47.320', W 122° 19.755'

GETTING THERE

Driving from Everett: Follow I-5 south to exit 179, then turn right onto 220th Street SW. Follow 220th Street SW for 0.3 mile and turn left onto 66th Avenue W. Continue south on 66th Avenue W (which becomes 65th Place W) for 1 mile. Then turn right onto Lakeview Drive and proceed for 0.6 mile to parking and trailhead at Ballinger Park on your left.

Driving from Seattle: Follow I-5 north to exit 178. Turn left onto 236th Street SW (which becomes Lakeview Drive) and proceed for 0.8 mile to parking and trailhead at Ballinger Park on your left.

Like its King County counterpart, Snohomish County's Interurban Trail follows an old trolley line for most of its way. Traversing parts of Edmonds, Mountlake Terrace, Lynnwood, and Everett, much of this trail will appeal primarily to bicyclists.

Interurban Trail through South Lynnwood Park

The trail currently includes several road and sidewalk sections and a stretch in South Everett that cannot be recommended because of safety concerns. However, the southern stretch from Edmond's Mathay-Ballinger Park to Beech Road near Lynnwood's Alderwood Mall makes for some decent walking and running.

GET MOVING

The best place to begin your southern Interurban Trail run or walk is from Ballinger Park. This former golf course on Lake Ballinger is now managed by the city of Mountlake Terrace. While the city is planning to eventually develop it with facilities and walking trails, you are currently free to explore it. It can get a little muddy during the wet months—and it's not an off-leash park, but you would never know it from all of the free-ranging dogs. If you're bringing your dog, please respect the park rules and other visitors.

From the park, walk on a wide sidewalk along Lakeview Drive (which becomes 228th Street SW) for 0.3 mile to the trail. Now decide—south or north. If you decide south, you'll

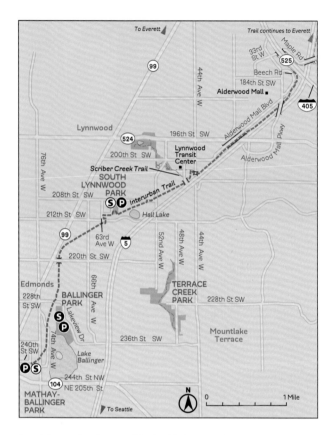

be able to check out a kiosk with interesting history displays. The trail south soon follows lightly traveled 74th Avenue W in a quiet neighborhood along Lake Ballinger. It then veers southwest as a bona fide trail coming to 76th Avenue W at 0.75 mile from 228th Street SW. Here, at the site of the historic Ballinger Station, take a break at a beautiful pergola and check out the historic displays.

From 1910 until 1939 much of this trail corridor served as a rail line for electric trolleys running between Seattle and

Everett. In essence a form of light rail, interurban lines serviced metropolitan areas all across America until automobiles eventually gained favor. This interurban line was the last to remain in service in Washington. Learn about the old trolley line and Lake Ballinger—named after Richard Ballinger, who owned the lake at one time and later became President Taft's secretary of the interior. The trail crosses the road and ends at the small Mathay-Ballinger Park (parking) in 0.25 mile. Perhaps someday the trail will connect with the Interurban Trail in Shoreline and Seattle.

If you decide to head north from 228th Street SW, here's what you can expect. The way follows alongside Hall Creek through an urban and suburban environment. There are some wetlands and big trees along the way and a couple of quiet street crossings. At 0.5 mile from 228th Street SW, the trail passes beneath busy 220th Street SW. It then leaves the creek and makes surface crossings of 216th Street SW and 66th Avenue W.

At 1.3 miles the trail comes to 212th Street SW. Following trail signs, walk or run a short distance here on 63rd Avenue W and 211th Street SW and pick up the trail once more in South Lynnwood Park (parking and restrooms). Pass the short trail that leads north to 208th Street SW. The Interurban Trail passes an attractive grove of tall firs and resumes its course on the old trolley bed once more. Pass Hall Lake, which is primarily out of view due to private residences, and cross 54th Avenue W, 208th Street SW, and 52nd Avenue W.

The trail then passes through a cut—one of only a couple along this route. At 2.6 miles the trail reaches the bustling Lynnwood Transit Center. This is a good spot to turn around—or perhaps head out to Scriber Lake (see Trail 1) on the Scriber Creek Trail, which takes off from the Lynnwood Transit Center.

If you want to continue on the Interurban Trail, take the pedestrian overpass over busy 44th Avenue W and then begin a long ascent paralleling often-clogged I-5. The way then parallels Alderwood Mall Boulevard, utilizing a long bridge to cross busy arterials and freeway ramps. It then descends, traveling between freeway and retail shops. Shortly after passing beneath 28th Avenue W, the trail comes to a temporary end on Beech Road at 4.4 miles from Ballinger Park. Call it quits here. Beyond, the trail travels on busy roads and along a busy freeway on its way to Everett, holding little appeal as a good running or walking route.

4 Terrace Creek Park

DISTANCE:	2 miles roundtrip
ELEVATION GAIN:	Up to 125 feet
HIGH POINT:	465 feet
DIFFICULTY:	Easy
FITNESS:	Walkers, runners
FAMILY-FRIENDLY:	Yes
DOG-FRIENDLY:	On leash
AMENITIES:	Restrooms, picnic tables, playground, disc-golf course
CONTACT/MAPS:	Mountlake Terrace Parks and Recreation; map not available online
GPS:	N 47° 47.203', W 122° 17.851'

3.16.19 (handwritten)

GETTING THERE

Driving from Everett: Drive I-5 south to exit 179. Turn left and drive 220th Street SW for 0.3 mile, then turn right onto 56th Avenue W and drive 0.9 mile. Turn left onto 236th Street SW and continue 0.4 mile. Then turn left onto 48th Avenue W and drive 0.2 mile to park and parking on your left.

Driving from Seattle: Drive I-5 north to exit 178. Turn right and follow 236th Street SW for 0.7 mile. Then turn left onto 48th Avenue W and drive north 0.2 mile to park and parking on your left.

Transit: Community Transit Route 111

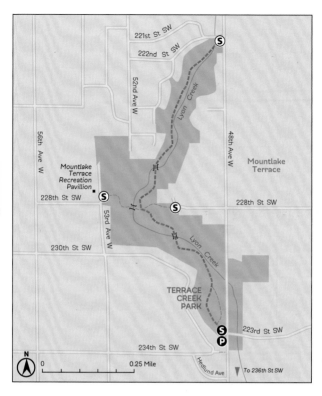

A pretty little greenbelt in the heart of suburban Mountlake Terrace, this 60-acre park protects a swath of forest alongside Lyon Creek. It also provides, for residents and visitors alike, wonderful outdoor recreation opportunities—including a well-maintained 1-mile trail. For walkers and runners, the trail is the most important aspect of this park, but others know this park for its challenging Frisbee golf course, picnic grounds, and playground. And it's the playground that is responsible for this park's sweet and Christmas-themed alternative name, Candy Cane Park.

Terrace Creek flowing alongside the trail

GET MOVING

Terrace Creek Park was established in the early 1950s, not too long after Mountlake Terrace's incorporation. The first playground piece installed in the park was painted with red and white stripes. Then, in 1956, according to Parks Services director, Ken Courtmanch, "the Lady Lyons Club donated two new metal play structures, consisting of a swing set and a two-level climber, making sure to keep the red and white painted theme. The children at the time affectionately called the park 'Candy Cane Park' and as they grew, their children continued the tradition."

By the late 1990s the original play equipment was replaced with new play structures. However, candy cane–themed equipment wasn't available, so the city purchased white swing sets and worked with a Boy Scouts of America troop who (using hundreds of rolls of tape) taped the swing sets and painted them to keep the candy cane theme alive.

For walkers and runners, the most important part of this park was created in 1969 with the purchase of several parcels along Lyon Creek forming a greenbelt north of the playground. To explore it, walk past the candy cane play equipment, following a paved path through a big field. Then meet up alongside the small creek and follow it upstream through a lush, emerald ravine. The area's original forest cover was logged long ago and you will see several big stumps testifying to the big trees that once grew here—but you'll walk past a few big trees in the mature second-growth forest that now flourishes.

The trail is a wide, soft-surfaced path marked with quarter-mile posts. At the halfway point, come to a junction. A wide path leads up out of the ravine to 228th Street SW, making for a nice loop via the sidewalk on 48th Avenue W back to your start. From this point, another path crosses the creek and climbs steeply left to the Mountlake Terrace Recreation Pavilion and off-leash dog park. There are some quiet, tree-lined streets and adjacent parks to walk through there as well.

The main trail continues up the ravine alongside the creek. During the wet months the added flow makes for a few nice little cascades. At 1 mile the trail terminates at 221st Street SW.

5   North Creek Park

DISTANCE:	2 miles roundtrip
ELEVATION GAIN:	30 feet
HIGH POINT:	250 feet
DIFFICULTY:	Easy
FITNESS:	Walkers, hikers
FAMILY-FRIENDLY:	Yes
DOG-FRIENDLY:	On leash
AMENITIES:	Restrooms, picnic tables, playground
CONTACT/MAPS:	Snohomish County Parks
GPS:	N 47˚ 49.950', W 122˚ 12.953'

GETTING THERE

Driving from Everett: Drive I-5 to exit 183. Then follow 164th Street SW (which becomes 164th Street SE) east for 1.7 miles to State Route 527. Turn right and follow SR 527 for 1.3 miles south to 183rd Street SE. Turn right and proceed west for 0.5 mile to park entrance on right.

Driving from Bellevue: Drive I-405 north to exit 26. Then follow SR 527 north for 2.5 miles, turning left onto 183rd Street SE. Continue 0.5 mile west to park on your right.

Transit: Community Transit Route 106 stops at corner of SR 527 and 180th Street SE. From there it is a 0.5-mile walk on 180th Street SE and 183rd Street SE to the park.

North Creek Park is an island of natural beauty surrounded by a sea of suburban development. This sprawling wetland, however, offers more than just a great place for nearby city folk to get a taste of nature. This 85-acre park protects ecologically important wildlife habitat and helps provide flood control by acting as a giant sponge. Bog comprises nearly all of the park. But have no worries hiking through this saturated landscape, for an extensive boardwalk system allows you easy and dry access across this semi-submerged preserve.

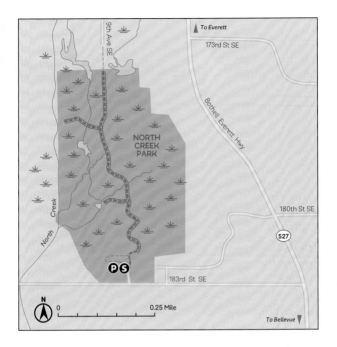

GET MOVING

Before hitting the trail, be sure to check out the information kiosk to get a better understanding of the terrain you are about to set foot on. Much of this area was once farmland: North Creek Park was part of the John Bailey Farm and some of that farm's structures still stand. The trail immediately leaves terra firma for a 0.75-mile-long boardwalk. Composed of more than 150 sections fitted together, this floating trail was extensively rebuilt not long ago.

Follow the floating boardwalk snaking across the expansive wetland meadow. Interpretive signs along the way provide insight into this special environment. Scrappy willows and a few lone hawthorns punctuate the grasses and reeds. Birdlife is prolific, especially in the spring. Red-winged blackbirds and

Hikers on North Creek Park's extended boardwalk

winter wrens fill the air with their melodious calls. As spring advances, sparrows, warblers, and vireos add their songs. Hawks are common, and you will frequently sight them hovering over the grasses searching for prey.

Herons are especially fond of North Creek Park too. A rookery exists in the park's northwest corner. In 0.3 mile a spur trail heads left for 500 feet, cutting through cattails and spirea to a peat bog. The main trail continues north through the wetlands complex. In another 0.25 mile another spur trail takes off to the left—this one leading 500 feet to a lookout close to the main creek channel. Look for beavers and muskrats swimming here in an open channel.

The main trail travels another 0.2 mile north to once again reach dry ground, and terminates a couple of hundred feet farther. Retrace your steps and enjoy the scene all over again, looking once more for creatures in the bog. This grassy swale of shallow water teems with life. Back at the trailhead, consider walking the short loop through the picnic area, where you'll be impressed with some large Sitka spruce trees.

6 North Creek Trail

DISTANCE:	4.8 miles roundtrip
ELEVATION GAIN:	140 feet
HIGH POINT:	380 feet
DIFFICULTY:	Easy
FITNESS:	Walkers, runners
FAMILY-FRIENDLY:	Yes
DOG-FRIENDLY:	On leash
AMENITIES:	Restrooms, picnic tables, playground, and pool at McCollum Pioneer Park
CONTACT/MAPS:	Mill Creek Facilities, Parks and Recreation
GPS:	N 47° 52.714', W 122° 13.254'

GETTING THERE

Driving: From Everett or Seattle drive I-5 to exit 186. Then head east on State Route 96 (128th Street SE) for 0.5 mile and turn right into McCollum Pioneer Park. Then proceed to the south end of the park and ride lot; the trail begins south of the parking lot.

Transit: Community Transit Routes 105, 106, 109, 115, 412, 810, and 860

Follow a lovely, winding paved path along the edge of a lush greenbelt embracing North Creek. From bustling McCollum Pioneer Park head out through groves of towering conifers skirting an array of residential complexes. Then emerge into the heart of Mill Creek's commercial district before returning to a tree-lined creekside route—finishing up at a duck-dabbling wetland pool.

North Creek Trail in Bothell

GET MOVING
Although this trail can be accessed from many places along its 2.4-mile span, the McCollum Pioneer Park Trailhead offers the best parking options, restrooms, direct bus access, and additional trails if you need more to explore.

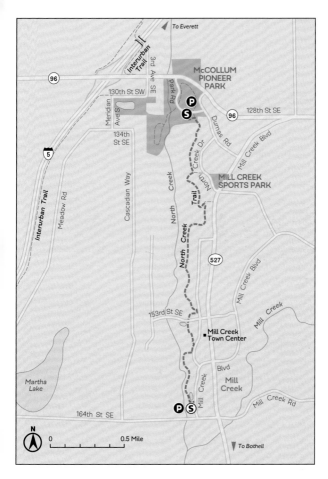

Locate the trailhead across the park loop road south of the park-and-ride parking area. The paved path immediately travels beneath a cool canopy of towering conifers. It then begins its gently rolling and winding course southward along a demarcation of suburban developments to the east and forested wetlands to the west. North Creek snakes through those wetlands, at times hidden from the trail, and other times close by.

Skirt apartments, townhouses, and condominiums, and bear right at a junction where a short trail leads left to sports fields. At 0.8 mile come to a quiet observation deck. The trail carries on, often lined with split-rail fences and graced with benches and interpretive signs. It is quite aesthetically appealing. In addition to the big conifers passed along the way, towering cottonwoods and pretty birches (especially in autumn) grow along the trail.

At 1.4 miles, just after passing an exceptional grove of tall trees, pass a couple of wetland pools. At 1.8 miles cross 153rd Street SE. The way then passes through the center of Mill Creek and crosses a small creek. A short spell on side-walks leads past restaurants and cafes that may tempt you to break your stride. You'll pass a running specialty store, too, where groups of runners often depart for social runs on the trail.

The trail makes a sharp right turn to head around some municipal buildings soon to meet up with North Creek. Here quiet spots along the creek tempt a break or picnic. The way eventually comes to some restored wetlands often teeming with avian life. At 2.4 miles the trail terminates on Mill Creek Boulevard. Parking is available at a nearby lot (note spaces reserved for trail users). The trail will eventually connect with existing trail farther south in North Creek Park (see Trail 5) and in Bothell farther south. Once completed, it will connect the Interurban Trail with the Sammamish Trail.

GO FARTHER

At McCollum Pioneer Park you can enjoy a leisurely walk on a half-mile paved path by the playfields, or take a 1-mile nature trail through a forest grove along North Creek.

The North Creek Trail in Bothell is definitely worth a visit. The best place to start your walk or run here is from the North

Creek Sportsfields near North Creek Parkway and 120th Avenue NE. Here follow a paved path 0.6 mile north to NE 195th Street. Cross the road and connect with a soft-surface path that follows a dike along North Creek. You can continue left to the UW Bothell campus or continue right on the main trail. There is another trail on the west bank of the creek. Several road crossings complete with bridges over the creek allow you to create some loop options.

The main North Creek Trail travels north coming to 240th Street SE at 1.5 miles. Here it parallels roads for 1 mile. It then crosses 228th Street SE and meanders about 0.8 mile across a large wetland greenbelt in the center of a very busy area of stores and offices. This section passes ponds and forests and includes some side trails, offering a respite from the surrounding commotion. The trail then crosses 220th Street SE and parallels 20th Avenue SE for about 0.5 mile to terminate on the Bothell Everett Highway. Government officials hope to soon continue this trail northward to connect with the existing trail sections. It will be quite a nice long-distance path once completed.

7 Paradise Valley Conservation Area

DISTANCE:	13 miles of trails
ELEVATION GAIN:	Up to 200 feet
HIGH POINT:	440 feet
DIFFICULTY:	Easy
FITNESS:	Hikers, runners, cyclists
FAMILY-FRIENDLY:	Yes, but note several trails are open to bikes and horses
DOG-FRIENDLY:	On leash
AMENITIES:	Restrooms
CONTACT/MAPS:	Snohomish County Parks
GPS:	N 47° 47.311', W 122° 04.751'

Stately second-growth in Paradise Valley

GETTING THERE

Driving: From State Route 522 in Maltby (6.5 miles east of Bothell; 8 miles west of Monroe), head east on Paradise Lake Road for 1.7 miles to the trailhead on your right.

Consisting of nearly 800 forested acres on the edge of suburbia along the King–Snohomish county line, Paradise Valley is not only hiking and running heaven but also a haven for wildlife. Originally homesteaded in the 1880s, Paradise Valley Conservation Area now provides refuge for bear, cougar, deer, and a myriad of other critters both furry and feathered. And the park also protects the headwaters of Bear Creek, an important salmon stream.

GET MOVING

Opened on Earth Day 2009, Snohomish County Park's 793-acre Paradise Valley Conservation Area has become one of the region's most popular hiking, mountain biking, and trail running destinations. With over 13 miles of trails currently in place and more yet to be constructed, there is plenty of ground at Paradise Valley to explore. Park officials also hope to build an educational facility sometime in the near future.

Before setting out, download a map or study the map of the park's extensive trail system at the kiosk at the main

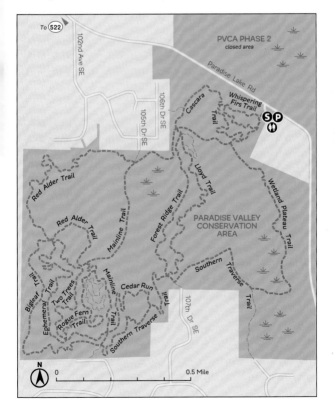

trailhead. Then have fun exploring this sprawling conservation area. Follow the 1.6-mile Mainline Trail through the core of the park to access other trails deeper within Paradise Valley. Traversing forests of fir and alder, the trail travels through old cuts, stands of mature timber, wetland flats, and a small ridge. While the hike out and back to the trail's terminus at the park's southern boundary certainly makes for a good afternoon jaunt, scores of opportunities exist to extend your adventure. A dozen-plus trails radiate from this main artery, including a few that are hiker-only. Below are a few suggested itineraries.

The hiker-only Whispering Firs Trail, complete with interpretive signs, makes a nice half-mile escape perfect for young hikers and older ones short on time. It is reached by following the Mainline Trail a short distance.

Follow the Mainline Trail for 1 mile. Then head right on the Red Alder Trail for 0.3 mile where the Bigleaf, Ephemeral, and Two Trees trails all depart southward. These three trails varying in distance from 0.8 mile to 1 mile can be combined to form loops. They lead past wetlands that burst with birds and blossom with wildflowers in the springtime.

Take the Mainline Trail 0.3 mile to a junction with the 0.6-mile hiker-only Forest Ridge Trail and 0.9-mile Lloyd Trail. Combine them for a good loop with a little bit of elevation gain, a long boardwalk bridge, and some nice trees, including rare western white pines.

For a grand 5-mile loop of the conservation area, follow the Mainline Trail for 0.1 mile. Then head right onto the 0.7-mile Cascara Trail. You'll then return to the Mainline Trail, where you'll want to head right 0.2 mile to the Red Alder Trail. Then embark right on this snaking trail coming to the Bigleaf Trail in 1 mile. Next follow the Bigleaf Trail 1 mile to the Southern Traverse Trail. Take this fun trail down into a ravine and across a long boardwalk—then up a ridge to a plateau. In 1.1 miles reach a junction with the Wetland Plateau Trail. Veer left onto this 0.8-mile trail, traveling along the edge of the plateau. Pass a few limited viewpoints, and enjoy a fair degree of solitude. Now finish the grand loop by turning right onto the Mainline Trail and traveling 0.1 mile back to the trailhead.

8 Big Gulch

DISTANCE:	2.7 miles of trails
ELEVATION GAIN:	Up to 400 feet
HIGH POINT:	500 feet
DIFFICULTY:	Easy to moderate
FITNESS:	Hikers, runners
FAMILY-FRIENDLY:	Yes
DOG-FRIENDLY:	On leash
AMENITIES:	Restrooms, picnic table, playground
CONTACT/MAPS:	Mukilteo Parks and Recreation
GPS:	N 47˚ 54.833', W 122˚ 17.816'

GETTING THERE
Driving: From Everett, follow I-5 south to State Route 526 (Boeing Freeway). Then continue west on SR 526 for 4.5 miles. Bear right onto 84th Street NW (which is still SR 526) and

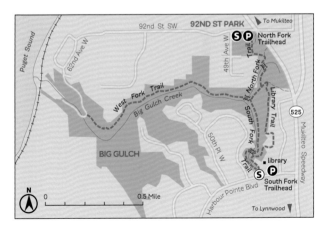

A pair of hikers on the North Fork Trail

continue 0.4 mile to SR 525. Then turn left (south) onto SR 525 (Mukilteo Speedway) and drive 0.5 mile to 92nd Street SW. Turn right and then immediately turn left into the 92nd Street Park parking area.

   Transit: Community Transit Routes 113, 417, 880

Once logged for its cedars and firs and slated for a massive refinery, today Big Gulch is a southern Snohomish County greenbelt graced with several miles of trails and offering some fairly decent roaming just minutes from busy Paine Field. The Mukilteo Parks Department, along with a slew of volunteers, have built and upgraded a decent trail system within this big green gully.

GET MOVING

Formally owned by the Port Gamble Lumber Company, Big Gulch and its surrounding bluffs were heavily logged in the early twentieth century—but a few big trees were left behind in the tight confines of the gulch. In the 1960s the Chevron Oil Company owned the land and proposed a refinery for it. By the 1980s it was slated for the Harbour Pointe development, which eventually became part of the city of Mukilteo. While homes and businesses replaced the second- and third-growth forests on the bluffs, Big Gulch and the Picnic Point Creek drainages (sometimes referred to as the Chevron parklands) remained green. The growing city finally decided to utilize the gulch for more than just a greenbelt and made it into a trail haven.

Locate the signed and arched North Fork Trailhead at the southeast corner of the 92nd Street Park. Walk a short distance, coming to a junction. The trail to the left heads back to the sidewalk along SR 525. The trail to the right, the North Fork Trail, utilizes sturdy steps dropping into the gulch—the trailwork here is top-notch. The ambience here is wild despite the fact that houses and businesses occupy the bluffs above. Throughout most of the gulch you are unaware of that!

Cross Big Gulch Creek on a nice bridge and soon come to a junction with an old road. The way left climbs 0.3 mile out of the gulch on its way to the Staybridge Suites, an alternative starting point. It also connects with the Library Trail offering a loop. Head right and at 0.3 mile from the trailhead come to a junction with the South Fork Trail at a big bridge.

You can continue right on the wide West Fork Trail, crossing the bridge and following a sewer line along Big Gulch Creek. Despite the occasional whiff of effluent, the area is pretty wild and the walking quite enjoyable. After crossing a boardwalk, the trail leaves the sewer line and begins to climb above the creek. On well-built trail, traverse steep slopes high above the creek. Pass a couple of viewpoints and slowly descend. Eventually catch a glimpse of the Sound before the trail terminates in 1 mile on a service road. Turn around here and retrace your steps to the South Fork Trail junction.

Now either return to the trailhead by going left or head right (south) following a tributary for 0.5 mile up and out of the gulch. This section of trail is very nice, passing big trees and small cascades in the tight gully. The way gradually reclaims lost elevation, ending its journey at the Mukilteo Library on Harbour Pointe Boulevard. You can either retrace your steps back to the 92nd Street Park or, for a loop, walk the Library Trail. This fairly new trail travels 0.6 mile along the gulch's rim, skirting businesses and coming to the old service road. Turn left here and head 0.1 mile to the North Fork Trail junction. Then march off right to return to your start, tackling those stairs again—this time going up.

9 Japanese Gulch Conservation Area

DISTANCE:	More than 7 miles of trails
ELEVATION GAIN:	Up to 500 feet
HIGH POINT:	540 feet
DIFFICULTY:	Easy to moderate
FITNESS:	Hikers, runners, cyclists
FAMILY-FRIENDLY:	Yes
DOG-FRIENDLY:	On leash
AMENITIES:	Restrooms, off-leash dog park
CONTACT/MAPS:	Mukilteo Recreation Department
GPS:	N 47° 56.786', W 122° 17.533'

GETTING THERE

Driving: From exit 192 on I-5 in Everett, head west on 41st Street for 0.7 mile. Then bear left onto W Mukilteo Boulevard. Now continue on this arterial (which becomes 5th Street in Mukilteo)

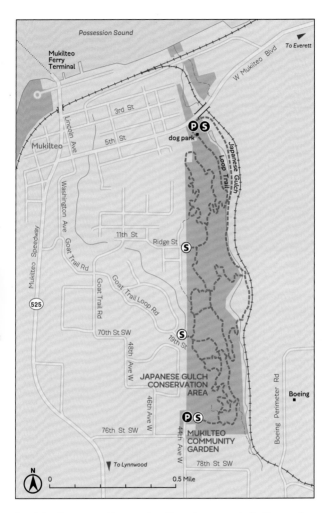

for 4.4 miles to parking and trailhead on your left. Alternative trailhead and parking are at the Mukilteo Community Garden, located at the junction of 76th Street SW and 44th Avenue W.

Old mill remains

Transit: Community Transit Route 113 stops on the Mukilteo Speedway. From there it is a 0.5-mile walk on 5th Street to the trailhead.

Straddling the Everett–Mukilteo city line and tucked between Paine Field and Possession Sound is a lush greenbelt harboring miles of trails and a fascinating history. A concerned citizens group helped convince the city of Mukilteo to purchase a large section of Japanese Gulch, once threatened with development, for a park. Volunteers have since been busy constructing trails in the gulch for hiking, mountain biking, and trail running.

GET MOVING

Japanese Gulch Conservation Area is laced with trails (many user-built and unofficial) and nearly all unsigned. Exploring the trails here can be confusing or fun—it's often both. A good introduction to this green oasis is the Japanese Gulch Loop

Trail, which begins next to the dog park. Follow this well-constructed trail under a thick forest canopy and begin traversing a steep slope above a tumbling creek.

The way passes a small old dam and spillway—remains of a lumber mill operation. This deep ravine once housed the Crown Lumber Company, which employed a large population of Mukilteo residents of Japanese descent (who were heavily discriminated against in other communities but found a home and employment here).

Beyond the dam, with the help of some steps, steeply climb to the 500-plus-foot rim of the gulch. The path bends north, allowing for some views through the trees of the Sound below before heading south. Ignore paths leading right to nearby neighborhoods. Pass several trails leading left back into the gulch. Any of them will work—but if you continue straight on the longest of the options you'll return to the gulch and an old road after about 2.2 miles. Then hike downhill on the old road following a cascading creek and returning to the trailhead after 1.2 miles.

You can veer off the loop by following an old woods road (now trail) to the upper parking lot at the Mukilteo Community Garden. Trailhead to trailhead, via the shortest route, is about 1.5 miles one-way and 500 feet of elevation gain. You can easily hike 5, 8, or even 10 miles here by making a series of interconnecting loops. There is also a lower Japanese Gulch Trail north of W Mukilteo Boulevard. It is about 0.25 mile long and connects to Mukilteo Lane.

The railroad tracks in the gulch as well as the slopes east of the tracks are private property. While Japanese Gulch is a favorite area for local hikers and runners, first-time visitors will probably have a hard time finding their way around. Hopefully the city and the volunteer Japanese Gulch Group will eventually upgrade some of the rougher paths and sign the trails and junctions. Of course, a good map would be nice too. In the meanwhile set your mood to intrepid!

10 Narbeck Wetland Sanctuary

DISTANCE:	1.8 miles of trails
ELEVATION GAIN:	Minimal
HIGH POINT:	525 feet
DIFFICULTY:	Easy
FITNESS:	Walkers, hikers
FAMILY-FRIENDLY:	Yes
DOG-FRIENDLY:	On leash on perimeter trail, prohibited on interior interpretive trail
AMENITIES:	Restrooms, interpretive signs, picnic tables
CONTACT/MAPS:	Friends of Narbeck Wetland Sanctuary; map not available online
GPS:	N 47° 56.056', W 122° 15.613'
BEFORE YOU GO:	Open 7:00 AM to dusk.

GETTING THERE

Driving: From Everett follow I-5 south to exit 189. Then drive State Route 526 west for 2.5 miles, exiting onto Seaway Boulevard. Proceed for 1 mile north. Entrance is on right, across the street from the Fluke Corporation.

The Narbeck Wetland Sanctuary sits in the heart of one of Everett's largest industrial areas, close to Paine Field. A mitigated wetland, the sanctuary is the result of a public and private partnership involving more than three hundred volunteers and $6 million. With the creation of this high-functioning, quality wetland, not only did birds and frogs get a great new place to hang out in Everett—hikers did too.

GET MOVING

Opened to the public in 1999, Narbeck is the product of wetland banking—that is, the creation of new wetlands to mitigate the loss of wetlands to development. In this case, Narbeck was created to offset the environmental loss of wetlands that were filled in to allow for the expansion of nearby Paine Field. This project became the first of its kind in Snohomish County.

Explore the wetlands by following the 1.5-mile Perimeter Trail (which partially utilizes sidewalks) and a 0.3-mile board-walk that winds through the wetland's interior. Children will especially enjoy the boardwalk. Crushed gravel tread and raised boardwalks require no fancy footwear for you to walk this saturated sanctuary.

The trails are short, but they invite lingering. Take time to read the attractive interpretive signage. Gaze through the alder thickets, cedar groves, and reeds for birds and amphibians. Buffleheads and mallards are abundant. Deer and beavers are occasionally sighted here too. Note the large cedar stumps. It may be hard to imagine that this little wildlife oasis stuck smack dab in the middle of industrial Everett was once covered in ancient forest.

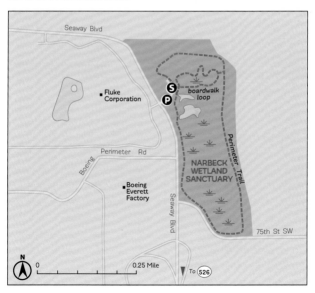

Narbeck's boardwalk trail

Although the walk through Narbeck is soothing and bird-song fills the air, you'll be hard-pressed to fully enjoy it with all of the industrial noise in the background. Still, if you cover your ears, your eyes may very well have you believing that you are far from the commotion. Try to time your visit early or late in the day when nearby shift workers aren't using the sanctuary for their lunch break workout. In any case, this natural retreat close to the population centers of Snohomish County makes for a great place to visit throughout the year—especially in the spring when life abounds at this manmade wetland sanctuary.

11 Forest Park

DISTANCE:	About 1.5 miles of trails
ELEVATION GAIN:	Up to 400 feet
HIGH POINT:	390 feet
DIFFICULTY:	Easy to moderate
FITNESS:	Walkers, runners
FAMILY-FRIENDLY:	Yes
DOG-FRIENDLY:	On leash
AMENITIES:	Restrooms, playground, water playground, animal farm, picnic shelters, swim center, ball courts
CONTACT/MAPS:	Everett Parks and Community Services
GPS:	N 47° 57.595', W 122° 13.287'
BEFORE YOU GO:	Park open 6:00 AM to 10:00 PM, April 1–Oct. 31; 6:00 AM to 8:00 PM, Nov. 1–March 31.

GETTING THERE

Driving: From exit 192 on I-5 in Everett, head west on 41st Street for 0.7 mile. Bear left onto E Mukilteo Boulevard. Continue on this arterial for 0.2 mile, turning left onto Park Road. Proceed 0.3 mile through the park to parking lots and trailheads.

Everett's oldest city park, Forest Park bustles with activity. Greatly enhanced during the Great Depression, the park was once home to a small zoo. Today it contains a popular animal farm and a swim center. But beyond the busy park facilities and picnic grounds are a series of short trails traversing groves of stately second-growth conifers. While short in distance, the trails offer quiet wanderings—and an excellent hill workout.

GET MOVING

Forest Park occupies more than 100 acres of hilly terrain. The main parking areas and park facilities pretty much sit atop

Stately conifers in Forest Park

the park's high point—meaning all of those radiating trails head downhill. And those downhills are steep, too, so you'll get your heart pumping coming back up them. The park published a hill challenge map (posted at the main kiosk) showing a course you can take to tackle all of the hilly trails leading north from the park center. The challenge is to see how fast you can complete them.

Except for the 0.25-mile Nature Trail loop, the trails aren't named or signed, but there are numbered posts and blocks at many of the intersections. An old access road now acts as a wide paved path. All of the other trails are soft surface. In

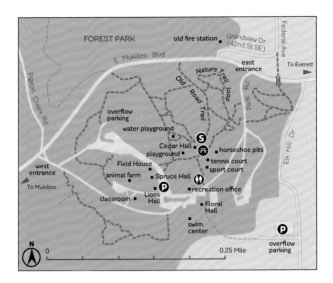

addition to the cluster of paths immediately to the north of the park's main area, there is another path that takes off west from the swim center and heads toward the west entrance. You can cross the park access road here and follow another trail that skirts an overflow parking area before returning to the main cluster.

An old service road now acts as a trail on the north side of E Mukilteo Boulevard, but there are no crosswalks or safe crossings of the busy road to access it. Trails do lead, however, to a pedestrian overpass across the busy boulevard near the park's east entrance. This leads to Grandview Drive and other quiet streets offering good walking routes to 41st Street, where you can continue east to bus stops on Rucker Avenue.

You can easily walk a mile or two by circumnavigating the main park area and making a few loops. And while the trail terrain is small compared to the rest of the park, mature conifers interspersed with some rhododendrons make it attractive. Forest Park is a great place to bring young hikers, as you can reward them later with a trip to the water playground or animal farm (open from late June to late August).

GO FARTHER
Not too far to the west via Mukilteo Boulevard and Olympic Boulevard is Everett's Howarth Park. This small park offers a half mile of trails on ravines and bluff tops as well as access to a small off-leash beach on Possession Sound.

12 Everett Waterfront Trail

DISTANCE:	6 miles of trails
ELEVATION GAIN:	Minimal
HIGH POINT:	40 feet
DIFFICULTY:	Easy
FITNESS:	Walkers, runners
FAMILY-FRIENDLY:	Yes
DOG-FRIENDLY:	On leash
AMENITIES:	Restrooms, concessionaires, historic sites, interpretive plaques, picnic tables
CONTACT/MAPS:	Port of Everett
GPS:	N 48° 00.252', W 122° 13.392'
BEFORE YOU GO:	Current construction projects may have sections of the trail temporarily closed.

GETTING THERE
Driving from Everett: From exit 193 on I-5 turn left onto Pacific Avenue, then immediately right onto Maple Street. Continue 0.4 mile north and turn left onto Everett Avenue (State Route 529). Continue west on Everett Avenue for 1.1 miles and turn right onto W Marine View Drive (still SR 529). Continue 1.5 miles north and turn left onto 10th Street. Then drive 0.3 mile to parking and trailhead.

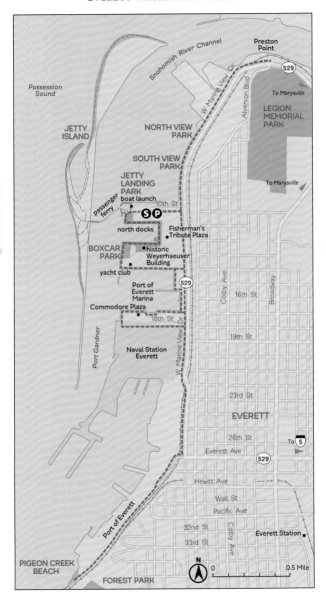

Everett Waterfront Trail in sunset's evening glow

Driving from Marysville: Take exit 198 off I-5 and follow SR 529 (which eventually becomes E Marine View Drive) 4.4 miles to 10th Street.

You can park for a fee at Jetty Landing Park from May 1 to September 30. Free parking is available along streets and at North View and South View parks. Be aware of car break-ins at North View and South View parks.

Views of the Olympic Mountains, marine mammal- and bird-watching, history exhibits, and a thriving pulse fueled by diners, boaters, fishermen and women, and naval personnel are what you can expect along the Everett Waterfront Trail. You can also expect to get in a good workout. The trail consists of 6 miles of paved paths and sidewalks that run from Pigeon Creek Beach all the way to Preston Point at the mouth of the Snohomish River.

GET MOVING

The Everett Waterfront Trail is actually a series of trails, with one main line extending along W Marine View Drive and several lines branching from it, traveling throughout a series of piers. The trail through the piers is known as the Waterfront Place Trail, or the "W," named after the shape of its route. It consists of a 3.5-mile journey (signed with half-mile markers) throughout the businesses, parks, and features comprising Waterfront Place. Waterfront Place is a 65-acre redevelopment currently transforming drab former industrial lands into a thriving new community of residences, restaurants, shops, and parks. There is a lot of construction activity taking place here, so expect some temporary trail section closures—and a lot of changes in general on return visits.

The best place along the Waterfront Trail for a walk is the W route. Accessible to jogging strollers and wheelchairs, this route passes some fascinating landmarks, including the site of the Everett Massacre (see "Everett Massacre" sidebar). It also passes the iconic, historic Weyerhaeuser Building, a 1923-built, 6000-square-foot Gothic-style building utilizing local wood products that once served as the offices for the company's mills along the waterfront.

The W starts at the Fishermen's Tribute Plaza, then passes the Weyerhaeuser Building and crosses Boxcar Park, home to a farmers market and other events. It then passes the yacht club, large marina, shops, restaurants (which will tempt you to stop), and residences. The W then skirts Naval Station Everett before turning left to travel along W Marine View Drive for about 0.6 mile and then turning left again along 10th Street. You'll pass the *Equator,* a historic sailing vessel once used by Scottish author Robert Louis Stevenson on some of his South Pacific voyages in the late 1800s. The trail then passes the Jetty Island passenger ferry terminal (see Trail 13) before closing the circuit.

EVERETT MASSACRE

On Sunday, November 5, 1916, the Everett waterfront was the scene of the bloodiest labor confrontation in Washington's history. It was here during the midst of a local depression and rising tensions between organized labor and the city's ruling and business classes that a skirmish broke out, resulting in several deaths, numerous injuries, and a slew of arrests, leading to a dramatic and well-publicized trial. It was a pivotal point for the Industrial Workers of the World (IWW), also known as the Wobblies—an inclusive and radical union that counted among its ranks immigrants, women, and African and Asian Americans.

On that fateful Sunday, two ships carrying three hundred Wobblies set sail from Seattle to Everett to support striking shingle-weavers. They were met at the docks by a mob of two hundred citizen deputies and hired thugs led by Snohomish County sheriff Donald McRae. The Wobblies were not allowed to disembark. Gunfire then erupted, resulting in the deaths of at least twelve men, including two deputies. More than two dozen were injured.

The ships returned to Seattle, where seventy-four Wobblies were arrested. A dramatic and lengthy trial followed while the governor sent National Guard troops to the city to maintain order. Ultimately the Wobblies were acquitted: a huge victory for the group that had been subjected to many injustices since its founding in 1905. It was a big win for the Wobblies, but shortly afterward their influence waned as World War I broke out and their socialist leanings were questioned during the concurrent Russian Revolution.

Mystique and unanswered questions still exist about the massacre more than one hundred years later. Controversial Sheriff McRae, who was elected with union support but later became a strongman for the city's industries, went into reclusion. His place and time of death are still unknown. Today, class struggles continue and the disparity of wealth in the Puget Sound has become even more pronounced than it was in 1916.

The W can get clogged with pedestrian traffic during busy periods, making it a less than ideal place to run. Your better option for running in this area is the Waterfront Trail along W Marine View Drive. From the trailhead follow the trail along

10th Street for a quarter mile or so, reaching the main path. From here you can run north nearly a mile, passing South and North View parks along the Snohomish River Channel, or run south 2.5 miles, passing the naval station and utilizing a viaduct before turning right to skirt along the working seaport—eventually reaching a paved trail terminating at Pigeon Creek Beach and viewpoint. Both directions offer good maritime views near their ends—and good bird-watching and sunsets too.

GO FARTHER

From the trail's northern terminus you can follow sidewalk for a short distance, then carefully cross W Marine View Drive to Alverson Boulevard and continue your walk at the manicured grounds of Legion Memorial Park.

13 Jetty Island

DISTANCE:	More than 2 miles of beach
ELEVATION GAIN:	Minimal
HIGH POINT:	10 feet
DIFFICULTY:	Easy
FITNESS:	Walkers
FAMILY-FRIENDLY:	Yes
DOG-FRIENDLY:	Dogs prohibited
AMENITIES:	Restrooms, picnic tables
CONTACT/MAPS:	Port of Everett
GPS:	N 48° 00.228', W 122° 13.676'
BEFORE YOU GO:	Summer weekends can be busy and the parks department limits the number of visitors.

GETTING THERE

Driving from Everett: From exit 193 on I-5 turn left onto Pacific Avenue, then immediately right onto Maple Street. Continue 0.4 mile north and turn left onto Everett Avenue (State Route

Walker enjoying a deserted beach on an overcast summer day

529). Continue west on Everett Avenue for 1.1 miles and then turn right onto W Marine View Drive (still SR 529). Continue 1.5 miles north and turn left onto 10th Street. Then drive 0.3 mile to parking near Jetty Landing Park.

Driving from Marysville: Take exit 198 off I-5 and follow SR 529 (which eventually becomes E Marine View Drive) 4.4 miles to 10th Street.

Jetty Island is accessible via a free passenger ferry from July 1 through Labor Day. Pick up a boarding pass (required) at the ferry kiosk. Consult the website for ferry schedule, reservation information (reservations available to Everett residents and groups), and for island rules and regulations. Be flexible on your return trip, as the ferry can take only eighty people at a time. You can park for a fee at Jetty Landing Park from May 1 to September 30.

Who would have guessed that one of the finest beaches in all of Snohomish County is in Everett? Not along the city's developed waterfront, but just off of it on Jetty Island—a 2-mile-long, sandy expanse that's reachable by a five-minute

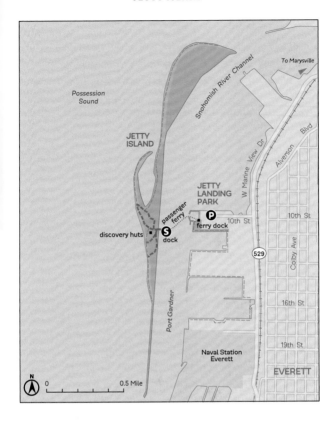

passenger ferry. And if it wasn't for Everett's industrial past and developed waterfront, there would be no Jetty Island. It was created by man, not nature.

GET MOVING

As you wait for the ferry, contemplate this island's interesting origin. Beginning in the 1890s, the Army Corps of Engineers built a jetty just north of Port Gardner—then commenced to dredge a channel. The spoils, along with silt and sedimentation from the Snohomish River, eventually created an island. It didn't take long for sand to accumulate from tidal movements. Plants began to colonize the island as well. Birds arrived and nested—and the island began taking on characteristics of a wild place. The city eventually realized this natural (albeit manmade) gem within its harbor. In the 1980s the Everett Parks and Community Services Department began providing passenger service to the island. Today over fifty thousand folks visit this sandy haven every summer.

Once you arrive on the island, walk past a restroom to a small picnic area and two discovery huts, the site of regular interpretive programs. To the left of this area a small interpretive nature trail takes off south across salt marshes. To the west of the huts and picnic tables a well-worn path passes by more tables and some volleyball courts to deliver you to the beach. And what a beach—especially during low tides when extensive sand flats reach into Possession Sound.

You can walk south on the beach to the jetty and north on the beach all the way to the mouth of the Snohomish River delta. A fairly large lagoon has developed just north of the island's recreation area that involves some channel crossing—unless you choose instead to walk around the bird-loving lagoon. And you'll see a lot of birds on the island—sandpipers, osprey, kingfishers, herons, finches, ducks, and more.

A few trees have taken root on Jetty, but it's mostly a place of little shade. You won't be able to walk around the island, as the channel side contains no beach, and the narrow interior of the island is cloaked in blackberry and other shrubs. But the beach is wide and smooth and you can easily walk 4 to 5 miles from tip to tip.

On a sunny day, soak in views of the Olympic Mountains; Whidbey, Camano, and Gedney islands; downtown Everett; and a backdrop of the Cascades. On an overcast day, savor the shadows on the sand and relative solitude, enjoying this peaceful place that lies just minutes away from Washington's seventh-largest city.

14 Langus Riverfront Park and Spencer Island

DISTANCE:	More than 5 miles of trails
ELEVATION GAIN:	Minimal
HIGH POINT:	10 feet
DIFFICULTY:	Easy
FITNESS:	Walkers, hikers, runners
FAMILY-FRIENDLY:	Yes
DOG-FRIENDLY:	Dogs prohibited on Spencer Island
AMENITIES:	Restrooms, picnic tables
CONTACT/MAPS:	Snohomish County Parks, Washington Department of Fish and Wildlife, and Everett Parks and Community Services
GPS:	N 48° 00.076', W 122° 10.587'
BEFORE YOU GO:	Langus Riverfront Park is open 6:00 AM to 10:00 PM, April 1–Oct. 31; 6:00 AM to 8:00 PM, Nov. 1–March 31.

GETTING THERE

Driving from Everett: Take exit 195 off of I-5, turning left onto E Marine View Drive. Then continue for 1.5 miles, turning left onto State Route 529 (Pacific Highway). Drive north on SR 529 for 0.5 mile, turning right onto 28th Place NE (signed for Langus Riverfront Park). Then immediately turn south onto Ross Avenue. Bear right at 0.4 mile onto Smith Island Road. At 1 mile, bear right at a Y intersection and continue another 0.4 mile to Langus Riverfront Park (more parking is located farther south).

Driving from Marysville: Take exit 198 off of I-5 and follow SR 529 south for 0.8 mile, exiting right onto 34th Avenue NE (Frontage Road). Drive 0.9 mile, bearing right onto Smith Island Road, then continue 1.4 miles to trailhead.

The Langus Riverfront Park on Smith Island in the Snohomish River delta is one of Everett's most popular running and

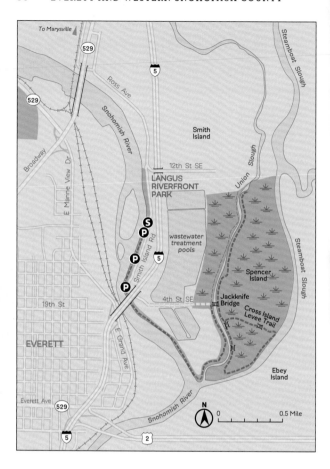

walking destinations. Here a trail travels along the Snohomish River, granting views south of Mount Rainier rising above the floodplain. The trail leads to a bridge to 400-acre Spencer Island, which sits in the heart of the Snohomish River Estuary, a wildlife-rich ecosystem where salt and fresh waters mix. Here trails follow snaking sloughs to a slew of scenic delights from glistening mudflats to glimpses of snowcapped

Langus Riverfront Trail along the Snohomish River

peaks. And the bird-watching is superb. **Note:** The Washington Department of Fish and Wildlife manages the northern half of the island, which is open seasonally to hunting.

GET MOVING

From any of the numerous parking areas within and just to the south of Langus Riverfront Park, start walking or running the park's paved 2.2-mile trail. The northern reaches of the trail traverse neatly landscaped park grounds. You're sure to see a lot of activity on the river, from waterfowl to local sculling crews. After passing beneath I-5 and traveling by a water treatment plant, the trail eventually bends north. Now traversing wilder surroundings, the path follows alongside Union Slough through groves of large Sitka spruces. The paved trail comes to an end at the old Jackknife Bridge to Spencer Island. You can continue running or hiking on Spencer Island's soft-surface trails.

From the bridge, the trail left follows a levee north to Washington Fish and Wildlife land, terminating in 1 mile. This land is open to hunting, so take that into consideration. The trail right is on Snohomish County Parks land and is closed to hunting (and to dogs). Continue a quarter mile south to a junction with the Cross Island Levee Trail. Here you can head left or right for a 1.7-mile loop. There's a small boardwalk loop near the Cross Island Levee Trail junction that you may want to check out when it's not flooded—which is frequently. Watch for wildlife throughout the island. Scan reeds, cattails, and sedges to discover a myriad of waterfowl and songbirds. Watch for hawks, herons, harriers, widgeons, and ruddy and wood ducks. Look too for bald eagles, river otters, coyotes, and deer. And enjoy the view east across the saturated flats to Mount Pilchuck and Three Fingers.

You can easily hike or run for more than 5 miles by combining the two areas. If you are just interested in exploring Spencer Island and skipping the riverfront trail, park near the I-5 overpass. Then walk east 0.6 mile on gravel 4th Street SE, passing Everett's water treatment plant and reaching the old Jackknife Bridge. It's a shorter route to the island but far less interesting and scenic.

15 Lowell Riverfront Park

DISTANCE:	4 miles roundtrip
ELEVATION GAIN:	Minimal
HIGH POINT:	15 feet
DIFFICULTY:	Easy
FITNESS:	Walkers, runners
FAMILY-FRIENDLY:	Yes, and wheelchair accessible
DOG-FRIENDLY:	On leash
AMENITIES:	Restrooms, benches
CONTACT/MAPS:	Everett Parks and Community Services
GPS:	N 47° 56.830', W 122° 11.324'
BEFORE YOU GO:	Park open 6:00 AM to 10:00 PM, April 1–Oct. 31; 6:00 AM to 8:00 PM, Nov. 1–March 31.

GETTING THERE

Driving: From exit 192 on I-5 in Everett, head east on 41st Street. Then immediately turn right (south) onto S 3rd Avenue and proceed for 0.6 mile. Bear left onto Junction Avenue (which

Snohomish River with Mount Pilchuck in the distance

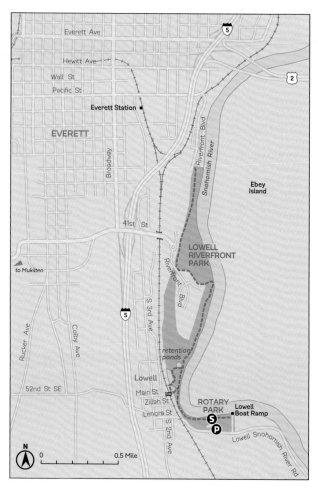

becomes S 2nd Avenue) and continue 0.6 mile to a four-way
stop. Turn left onto Lenora Street (which becomes Lowell Snohomish River Road), cross railroad tracks, and in 0.2 mile come
to the Lowell Riverfront Park on your left. (Additional parking is
available at Rotary Park 0.25 mile farther east).

Walk or run on a level, paved path along a big bend in the Snohomish River and through a corner of Everett rich in history. Enjoy good views to farmlands and old homes across the river on Ebey Island—and when the sun is out, of Mount Baker hovering in the distance. This trail has recently been expanded northward, allowing for even more riverfront rambling.

GET MOVING

The town of Lowell was long ago absorbed into Snohomish County's largest city, Everett. Founded in 1871 on a big bend on the Snohomish River, Lowell was named after a planned mill city in Massachusetts synonymous with industrialization. And while Snohomish County's entire population at the time was less than a thousand people, entrepreneurs and industrialists in Washington Territory had big plans for the region. The area's big timber and navigable river made it a choice spot for a sawmill.

Eventually, Lowell would boast a large pulp and paper mill. The mill, like many others within the Pacific Northwest, succumbed to changing market influences and was shut down. By the 1980s all that was left of the mill site was industrial waste—but the local Rotarians saw in the old mill site an opportunity to restore a landscape and turn it into a beautiful riverfront park. They donated much money and labor cleaning out the area so that it would be suitable for a park. Money was secured by the city to build the initial 1.5-mile paved trail along the river through the former industrial site. Volunteers continue to clean up the area, replacing invasive species with native ones.

From the trailhead, walk 0.25 mile upriver (east) beneath towering cottonwoods to Rotary Park. A popular spot for launching boats into the river, it is hard to imagine now the industrial activity that once flourished here. Now retrace your steps and head downriver toward the old pulp mill site. The path hugs the Snohomish River at the Lowell Bend, heading along grassy lawns punctuated with birch groves and columns of stately cottonwoods. Openings along the riverbank reveal weathered barns and productive farms on Ebey Island in the Snohomish River delta. On clear days, gaze out across the river to a backdrop of snowy, craggy Cascades peaks: Mount Pilchuck, Three Fingers, and Mount Baker among them.

The trail eventually bends left to where the old mill once stood. A new housing development now occupies this former blighted site and new landscaping and railings grace the trail here. The trail comes to Riverfront Boulevard, where you can turn right and pick up a brand-new section of trail. Follow this half-mile, paved path across wetlands and along the river to another new housing development on Riverfront Boulevard. Then retrace your steps.

For a diversion on your return, amble along retention ponds established in the late 1990s as part of the I-5 widening project. Soft-surface trails snake through naturally landscaped grounds housing reflecting pools. Head on over to a pedestrian-only bridge connecting the wetland restoration area and the riverfront trail to the Lowell business district. The bridge is an architectural marvel with its own waterfall. The steps will give you an added workout. And the entire area doesn't look too bad now considering its industrial past!

16   Lord Hill Regional Park

DISTANCE:	More than 30 miles of trails
ELEVATION GAIN:	Up to 1000 feet
HIGH POINT:	650 feet
DIFFICULTY:	Easy to moderate
FITNESS:	Hikers, runners, cyclists
FAMILY-FRIENDLY:	Yes, but trails shared with mountain bikes and equestrians

Lord Hill's Beaver Lake

May 19- 2019
3 hrs
10-1:00

DOG-FRIENDLY:	On leash
AMENITIES:	Restrooms
CONTACT/MAPS:	Snohomish County Parks and Recreation
GPS:	N 47° 51.553', W 122° 03.475'
BEFORE YOU GO:	Open 7:00 AM to dusk.

GETTING THERE

Driving: From Everett, head east on US Highway 2 for 8 miles and take the 88th Street SE exit. Turn right onto 88th Street SE (which eventually becomes 2nd Street) and drive 0.6 mile. Then turn left onto Lincoln Avenue, which becomes the Old Snohomish–Monroe Highway, and drive for 2.7 miles. Next turn right onto 127th Avenue SE and proceed for 1.6 miles to the park entrance and trailhead on your left.

Pocket wilderness, backyard wilderness, urban wilderness— all are appropriate descriptions of the sprawling forested ridge between the cities of Snohomish and Monroe known as Lord Hill Regional Park. More than 1450 acres of this emerald

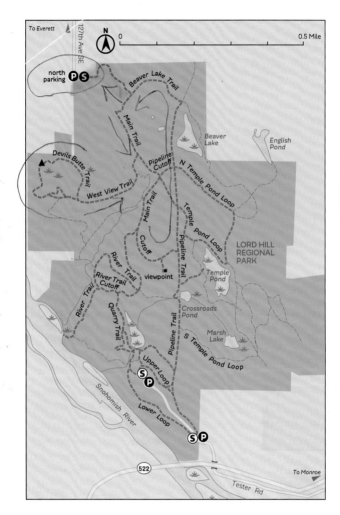

upland along the Snohomish River are protected from development within Snohomish County's Lord Hill Regional Park,
providing excellent hiking and running opportunities close to
the county's ever-growing population centers.

GET MOVING

The largest county park in Snohomish County, Lord Hill Regional Park consists of thickly forested slopes, lush ravines, wetland ponds, a couple of viewpoints, and a wild stretch of the Snohomish River. Its large and varied habitats also support a wide array of wildlife, including bear, cougar, and bobcat. There are more than 30 miles of trails and several miles of old woods roads traversing this park, named for Mitchell Lord, who homesteaded here in the 1880s.

A lot of loop options exist, from short leg stretchers to all-day explorations. However, the trails are poorly marked and can be confusing to follow. Carry a map (available online) or stick to the main trails, which are primarily old roads and are fairly well marked. Note that this park is popular with equestrians and mountain bikers too—so plan to share the trail. There are some hiker-only trails within the park. Here are four good suggestions to explore the park from the main trailhead. More options exist from the two southern trailheads accessed from Tester Road (from Monroe).

BEAVER LAKE LOOP

The Beaver Lake Loop provides 2.2 miles of hiking with 200 feet of elevation gain. Head down the Main Trail through a cool forest of big trees and over a series of boardwalks (slick when wet) coming to a junction in 0.4 mile. Turn left on the Beaver Lake Trail and follow it through a tunnel of alders to a junction. Turn right here on the Pipeline Trail and soon come to the marshy body of water called Beaver Lake. Continue on the Pipeline Trail and take a right on the Pipeline Cutoff Trail. Then take another right onto the Main Trail and return to the parking lot.

WEST VIEW LOOP

Another loop option is the West View Loop—3 miles of hiking with 400 feet of elevation gain. Head down the Main Trail through a cool forest of big trees and over a series of board-walks (slick when wet) coming to a junction in 0.4 mile. Now turn right, following the Main Trail for 0.4 mile to another junction. Here, turn right onto the West View Trail. After 0.8 mile come to a 650-foot knoll with a window view that includes Mount Baker. Take the short loop trail back to the West View Trail and retrace your steps back to the parking lot. You can extend this hike by 0.7 mile by heading up the Devils Butte Trail, which branches off of the West View Trail.

TEMPLE POND

Temple Pond provides 3.5 miles of hiking with 300 feet of elevation gain. From the Pipeline and Pipeline Cutoff junction (see Beaver Lake Loop above) head east on the N Temple Pond Loop. Follow this delightful trail for 1.2 miles, making a few dips, passing through an attractive forest grove, and traveling along the northeast shoreline of Temple Pond, the largest body of water within the park. The trail returns to the Pipeline Trail. From here, proceed east onto another Pipeline Cutoff trail—then head right on the Main Trail back to your start.

SNOHOMISH RIVER

The trek to the Snohomish River is 5 miles roundtrip with 800 feet of elevation gain. Head down the Main Trail through a cool forest of big trees and over a series of boardwalks (slick when wet) coming to a junction in 0.4 mile. Turn right, continuing on the Main Trail for 1.3 miles and avoiding all side trails. Now head right on the River Trail, dropping several hundred feet in 0.8 mile to a quiet and secluded spot on the Snohomish River. Retrace your route or follow the River Trail Cutoff to the Pipeline Trail to the Beaver Lake Trail back to your vehicle for a loop and a more varied and slightly longer return.

17 Bob Heirman Wildlife Preserve at Thomas Eddy

DISTANCE:	1.5 miles roundtrip
ELEVATION GAIN:	50 feet
HIGH POINT:	65 feet
DIFFICULTY:	Easy
FITNESS:	Hikers
FAMILY-FRIENDLY:	Yes
DOG-FRIENDLY:	Prohibited
AMENITIES:	Restrooms, picnic tables
CONTACT/MAPS:	Snohomish County Parks and Recreation
GPS:	N 47° 51.604', W 122° 05.547'
BEFORE YOU GO:	Open 7:00 AM to dusk.

GETTING THERE

Driving: From the city of Snohomish, travel south on State Route 9 for 2.6 miles to the junction with SR 96 (Lowell-Larimer Road). Turn left here onto Broadway Avenue, and after 0.8 mile bear left onto Connelly Road. Continue for another 0.8 mile to the preserve parking area and trailhead located on your left.

Walk across the Snohomish River floodplain, admiring the big river itself and oxbow ponds that teem with wildlife. In winter, marvel at the river churning with a voluminous flow; in summer, amble upon a wide gravelly bank. The preserve is one of the best places in Snohomish County for bird-watching; it harbors not only wintering trumpeter swans but scores of other species as well. Herons, harriers, ducks, mergansers, eagles, hawks, sandpipers, woodpeckers, swallows, warblers, tanagers, orioles, and goldfinches can all be spotted here.

Shadow Lake

GET MOVING

One of the prettiest and wildest spots along the Snohomish River, the 343-acre Bob Heirman Wildlife Preserve at Thomas Eddy nearly met a much different fate than the preservation it enjoys today. For many years, Teamsters Union president Dave Beck Jr. ran a gravel mine at the eddy. He then sold the property to a family that raised livestock on the surrounding floodplain. After that operation, plans were made to subdivide this flood-prone property into a large housing development, which would have been devastating to the thousands of migratory birds that use this river stretch for wintering and a big blow to the anglers that used this property to catch steelhead. The Snohomish Sportsmen Association, led by Bob Heirman, rallied to have this property preserved, ultimately leading to its acquisition by Snohomish County Parks. This

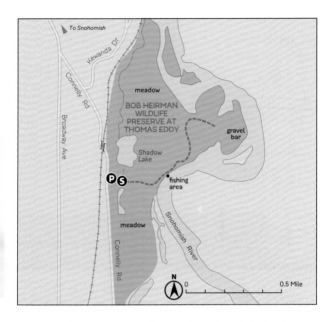

was not only great news to the area's anglers, but also to area bird-watchers and hikers.

Most of the property is floodplain and during the winter months is saturated. So stay on the main trails and avoid the preserve when flooded. From the trailhead follow an old road now serving as the preserve's central trail down a short but steep bluff to wetlands abutting the Snohomish River. Here a short (and overgrown) side trail takes off left to the cloud-reflecting oxbow pond called Shadow Lake. It teems with birdlife—so pack the binoculars—and during the winter months it bursts with ducks, grebes, and swans. Another smaller pond to the right of the main trail also teems with avian activity.

The main trail continues across marshy meadows to a dike. Here the way bends left and follows alongside the Snohomish River, continuing downstream with good views north across the river toward Lord Hill, another wonderful county park (see Trail 16). The trail here may be somewhat grown over—so consider wearing long pants as you work your way through the emerging jungle. Also, recent flooding has deposited some very large logs across the trail in one section, requiring some use of hands and extra oomph to negotiate them.

The trail then bends right to traverse a damp poplar flat and groves of large cottonwoods, reaching a sprawling gravel flat along the river at Thomas Eddy. When the river flow is low, take time to explore the shoreline here, and break out your bird guide to see what you can identify.

18   Centennial Trail

DISTANCE:	29.5 miles one-way
ELEVATION GAIN:	Up to 800 feet
HIGH POINT:	340 feet
DIFFICULTY:	Easy
FITNESS:	Walkers, runners
FAMILY-FRIENDLY:	Yes, jogging stroller– and wheelchair-friendly; note shared use with bicycles
DOG-FRIENDLY:	On leash
AMENITIES:	Restrooms, concessionaire, historic sites, interpretive plaques, picnic tables, benches
CONTACT/MAPS:	Snohomish County Parks
GPS:	N 47° 54.936', W 122° 05.285'
BEFORE YOU GO:	There is no parking at trail's actual start on 1st Street in Snohomish; parking is plentiful along Maple Avenue near Pine Avenue.

GETTING THERE

Driving to Snohomish Trailhead: From Everett follow US Highway 2 east for 8 miles. Then take the 88th Street SW exit and turn right. Follow 88th Street SW (which becomes 92nd Street SW, and finally 2nd Street upon crossing the Pilchuck River) for 1 mile. Then turn right onto Pine Avenue and drive

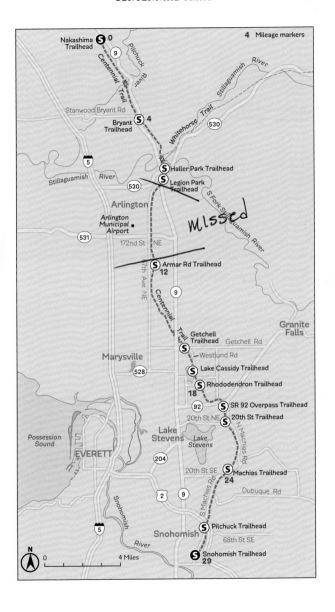

Nakashima Trailhead (S) 0

Pilchuck River

Centennial Trail

9

Stillaguamish River

Whitehorse Trail

Stanwood Bryant Rd

Bryant Trailhead (S) 4

530

5

(S) Haller Park Trailhead

Stillaguamish River

(S) Legion Park Trailhead

530

Arlington

S Fork Stillaguamish River

Arlington Municipal Airport

Missed

531

172nd St NE

9

(S) Armar Rd Trailhead 12

9

Centennial Trail

Granite Falls

(S) Getchell Trailhead   Getchell Rd

Marysville

Westlund Rd

528

(S) Lake Cassidy Trailhead

(S) Rhododendron Trailhead

18

92

(S) SR 92 Overpass Trailhead

20th St NE   (S) 20th St Trailhead

Possession Sound

Lake Stevens

Lake Stevens

N Machias Rd

EVERETT

204

20th St SE   (S) Machias Trailhead 24

2   9

Dubuque Rd

5

S Machias Rd

Snohomish River

(S) Pilchuck Trailhead

Snohomish   68th St SE

(S) Snohomish Trailhead 29

N

0   4 Miles

4 Mileage markers

Centennial Trail spanning the Stillaguamish River at Arlington

0.2 mile. Turn left onto 4th Street and proceed 0.1 mile to trailhead parking at the Snohomish Senior Center. **Note:** Parking is limited at the Snohomish Senior Center.

Driving to Nakashima Trailhead: From Everett follow I-5 north for 18 miles to exit 212. Then head east on Stanwood Bryant Road for 4.1 miles to Bryant at the junction with State Route 9 (trailhead parking also available here). Turn left and follow SR 9 for 4.3 miles to trailhead at Nakashima Heritage Barn and Centennial Trail North.

Other Trail Access Points: Additional trailheads with parking are located (south to north); Pilchuck (5801 S Machias Road, Snohomish), Machias (1624 Virginia Street, Snohomish), 20th Street (13205 20th Street NE, Lake Stevens), SR 92 Overpass (3651 127th Avenue NE, Lake Stevens); Rhododendron (10911 54th Place NE, Lake Stevens), Lake Cassidy—disabled parking only (6216 105th Avenue NE, Lake Stevens), Getchell (8318 Westlund Road, Arlington), Armar Road (1533 67th Avenue NE, Arlington), Legion Park (114 N Olympic

Avenue, Arlington), Haller Park (1100 W Avenue, Arlington), and Bryant (SR 9 and Stanwood Bryant Road, Arlington).

Transit: Community Transit Routes 270, 271, 277 stop near Snohomish Trailhead. Route 280 stops near 20th Street Trailhead. Routes 220, 230 stop near Legion Park Trailhead.

One of Snohomish County's most loved trails, the Centennial Trail was once a railroad line. Today the paved Centennial Trail runs for 29.5 miles from near the Snohomish River in the city of Snohomish to a historic farm on the Skagit County border. With a dozen developed trailheads, this county-spanning rail-trail can easily be accessed from Arlington, Marysville, Lake Stevens, and Snohomish. The trail skirts these bustling communities, traversing farmlands, forests, and wetlands and forming a de facto demarcation between suburbia and the rural countryside.

GET MOVING

Built in 1889, the year Washington became a state, the Seattle, Lake Shore, and Eastern Railroad line (later Northern Pacific, then Burlington Northern) remained partly in operation until 1987. Two years later, in 1989, local civic leaders and county parks personnel began transforming the decommissioned railway into the Centennial Trail. The trail has since grown to more than 29 miles long, with future plans to expand it north through Skagit County and south to King County to connect with the Sammamish Trail.

While cyclists certainly enjoy doing the entire trail in one fell swoop (an out-and-back ride makes nearly a metric century), pedestrians will want to sample sections at a time. Of course, it is also not unusual for ultrarunners to do the whole trail in a day. In general, the southern half is much busier than the northern half, and the prettiest sections of the trail, replete with pastoral settings, lie north of Arlington and just north of Snohomish. There are good views of Mount Pilchuck and Three Fingers Mountain along the way too. Paralleling sections of soft-surface trail are available for equestrians—but pedestrians can certainly use them too.

Below is a brief description of the trail from south to north.

From the Snohomish Trailhead, you can go south a few blocks if you care to see where the trail stops short of the Snohomish River—otherwise start north, eventually leaving the Snohomish city limits and traversing fields and forest along the Pilchuck River. At 2.1 miles (from the Snohomish Trailhead) come to the Pilchuck Trailhead. The trail continues north. Use caution crossing S Machias Road.

At 4.8 miles come to the Machias Trailhead, a lovely spot with its picnic and rest area (water available) graced with a replica of the 1890s depot station that once stood there. The trail then traverses fields before paralleling N Machias Road for some distance. It next goes through Lake Stevens, coming to the 20th Street Trailhead at 7.1 miles and the SR 92 Overpass Trailhead at 8.3 miles.

As the trail leaves the floodplain, it gains some elevation (albeit not much), and traverses forest and rural countryside. At 10.7 miles pass the Rhododendron Trailhead. At 11.2 miles pass the Lake Cassidy Trailhead (disabled parking only) and take a break at Lake Cassidy, where a nice little nature trail leads to a dock in the lake.

At 12 miles come to the popular Getchell Trailhead, then duck under SR 9 and begin a long descent, coming to the Armar Road Trailhead in 17 miles. The trail here utilizes a wide sidewalk, passing by housing developments and light industrial areas on its way to downtown Arlington. The trail goes right through old town Arlington (good place to stop for a bite to eat), passing by the Legion Park Trailhead and shortly afterward, at 21.1 miles, the Haller Park Trailhead.

Cross the South Fork Stillaguamish River on a restored trestle and pass the western terminus of the Whitehorse Trail, a 27-mile soft-surface trail that heads east to Darrington. The

NAKASHIMA FARM

The northern trailhead of Snohomish County's Centennial Trail sits on what was once a 1282-acre dairy farm operated by a Japanese American family. It was one of the few such farming operations in the county owned and operated by Americans of Japanese descent. And like most of these farms throughout Western Washington, the owners would permanently lose the farm, as a result of President Franklin D. Roosevelt's Executive Order 9066.

The Nakashima Farm has an interesting and somber history. Farming operations began here shortly after the turn of the twentieth century by Daniel Waldo Bass and his wife, Sophie, whose grandfather was A. A. Denny, the "Father of Seattle." In 1937 Bass sold the farm to Japanese American Takeo Nakashima. With the assistance of his family, Nakashima continued the dairy operation on the property.

However in 1942, after the Japanese bombing of Pearl Harbor, the Nakashima family was sent to internment camps in Idaho and California and was forced to sell its farm. In 1997 the Trust for Public Land purchased 89 acres of the farm and turned it over to the county for a park. In 2007 the barn was listed on Washington's heritage barn register, becoming the state's first and only one (so far) belonging to an Asian American farming family. It stands as a reminder, too, of one of our nation's most notorious civil rights violations.

The farm once encompassed more than 1200 acres, and most of the surrounding land is still rural. The county park preserves mainly wetland meadows. Most of the land west of the park is thick timber belonging to the Pilchuck Tree Farm and is managed for sustainable forestry, recreation, and wildlife. The county hopes to someday add more interpretive displays to the barn.

trail then climbs, soon skirting Bryant Lake and reaching the Bryant Trailhead at 25 miles. It next crosses SR 9 and traverses its wildest section, where a bear or two may be spotted. The trail crosses the Pilchuck River on a big bridge, skirts the Pilchuck Tree Farm, and terminates at 29 miles at the Nakashima Trailhead. Plan to spend some time here checking out the historic barn (see "Nakashima Farm" sidebar).

If you're inclined to do more walking or running, an unpaved and lightly traveled section of trail continues north, terminating in 1.4 miles near Lake McMurray in Skagit County.

19 | Lake Tye Park

DISTANCE:	1.6 miles roundtrip
ELEVATION GAIN:	Minimal
HIGH POINT:	30 feet
DIFFICULTY:	Easy
FITNESS:	Walkers, runners
FAMILY-FRIENDLY:	Yes, and jogging stroller- and wheelchair-friendly
DOG-FRIENDLY:	On leash
AMENITIES:	Restrooms, picnic tables and shelters, water, sports fields, beach
CONTACT/MAPS:	Monroe Parks and Recreation
GPS:	N 47˚ 51.531', W 122˚ 00.761'

GETTING THERE

Driving: From Everett follow US Highway 2 east for 12.7 miles. As you enter Monroe, turn right at the first traffic light onto

Lake Tye

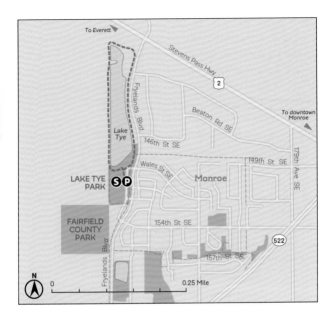

Fryelands Boulevard. Continue for 0.7 mile to the junction with Wales Street SE. Turn right into a large parking area and trailhead.

Transit: Community Transit Route 271

Walk or run around a small lake on the border between agricultural lands and suburbia. The trail is paved and level, making it ideal for folks of all fitness levels. Lake Tye Park is a great place for an early-morning or late-evening run or walk year-round. But it is particularly pleasing in autumn, thanks to its landscaping of eastern and European hardwoods.

GET MOVING

The city of Monroe has seen explosive growth since State Route 522 was built to the town in the early 1970s. A sleepy city of 2700 in 1973, Monroe is now a bustling residential and commercial center of nearly 20,000. Once surrounded by extensive dairy farms, the growing city has replaced many of its cow pastures with tract housing. But at Lake Tye Park on the western edge of Monroe, you can still catch a glimpse of the region's agricultural heritage. Situated on the sprawling Snohomish County floodplain, Lake Tye Park buffers new development from further encroachment upon some of the last remaining farmland in the valley. The 60-acre park was established as mitigation for recent development: in exchange for allowing high-density housing to be built within the city limits, Monroe residents gained a wonderful park complete with playfields, a swim area, and trails—important for runners and walkers.

A 1.6-mile paved trail circumnavigates 42-acre Lake Tye. The trail is lined with Norway maples and European sycamores, which add brilliant colors to the landscape come autumn. The park is also a good place for bird-watching. Moorhens, cormorants, and herons are year-round residents, while geese, grebes, swans, and other waterfowl make seasonal visits. If you desire a longer walk, several paths (paved and gravel) extend east and south through the adjacent neighborhood, connecting to several community parks and greenbelts.

20 Al Borlin Park

DISTANCE:	About 1.5 miles of trails
ELEVATION GAIN:	Minimal
HIGH POINT:	30 feet
DIFFICULTY:	Easy
FITNESS:	Walkers, runners
FAMILY-FRIENDLY:	Yes
DOG-FRIENDLY:	On leash
AMENITIES:	Restrooms, picnic tables and shelters, water, benches, playground

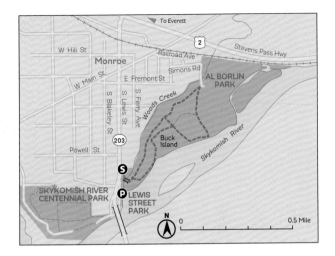

CONTACT/MAPS: Monroe Parks and Recreation
GPS: N 47° 51.531', W 122° 00.761'
BEFORE YOU GO: Trail is prone to flooding during periods of heavy rain. Homeless encampments and drug use are a concern here; exercise caution.

GETTING THERE

Driving: From Everett follow US Highway 2 east for 14.6 miles to Monroe. Turn right onto State Route 203 (S Lewis Street) and proceed south past the W Main Street traffic lights. At 0.8 mile turn left into the Lewis Street Park. Here you will find parking and the trailhead for Al Borlin Park.

Al Borlin Park sits along the Skykomish River at its confluence with Woods Creek. Within this 90-acre natural area is a peninsula called Buck Island, which during floods indeed becomes an island. Trails meander through the park, along river and creek banks and beneath a canopy of towering maples and cottonwoods. A few Sitka spruce can be found growing here too. There are also good viewing areas along the Skykomish River for observing birds and salmon.

Hiker enjoying an autumn day in Al Borlin Park

GET MOVING

Locate the trailhead within the lovely Lewis Street Park, Monroe's oldest park. The trail leads to a sturdy bridge spanning Woods Creek and then reaches a grassy picnic area at the confluence of Woods Creek and the Skykomish River. Contrast the two waterways: the Skykomish is a classic Northwest river, while Woods Creek looks more like it belongs in the Louisiana bayou country. Walk on an old gravel road—now a trail along the Skykomish River—taking in great views of one of Snohomish County's most important waterways. When the river levels are low, you can venture out onto some gravel bars.

Soon come to a junction. You can walk left through the heart of the island under a canopy of big hardwoods (quite showy in October), or continue right along the river, eventually coming to a parking area (access from Simons Road) usually filled with rigs of hopeful anglers. From here you can retrace your steps or walk the fishing access road to return on one of the two interior trails, which will guide you back to your start. The park isn't terribly large, so feel free to just amble and walk in circles if you wish!

In your wanderings you may notice remains of an old railroad trestle. At one time, the longest covered railroad bridge in the world traversed the Skykomish River at Buck Island. The 450-foot bridge was replaced in the 1960s with a new bridge, which was permanently dismantled in 2005. Old-timers may recall when Buck Island was a bustling place with passing freight trains. Now, however, the island is a pretty peaceful place.

GO FARTHER

Not too far to the west of Al Borlin Park is the Skykomish River Centennial Park. Within this park's 32 acres is a 1-mile paved perimeter path and an off-leash dog park. The park is accessed by following W Main Street west to Village Way, then south to the Sky River Parkway.

21 Osprey Park

DISTANCE:	2 miles of trails
ELEVATION GAIN:	Minimal
HIGH POINT:	125 feet
DIFFICULTY:	Easy
FITNESS:	Walkers, runners
FAMILY-FRIENDLY:	Yes
DOG-FRIENDLY:	Yes, on-leash and off-leash area
AMENITIES:	Restrooms, sports fields
CONTACT/MAPS:	Sultan Parks and Recreation
GPS:	N 47° 52.141', W 121° 49.299'

A silted channel on a rainy spring day

GETTING THERE

Driving: From Everett, follow US Highway 2 east for 22 miles to Sultan. Turn left onto 3rd Street and drive 0.6 mile north. Then turn left onto High Avenue and continue 0.1 mile to Osprey Park for trailhead and parking.

Wander on a series of wide, well-constructed, and interconnected trails through a mature forest of towering cedars, Sitka spruces, Douglas firs, and cottonwoods along the churning Sultan River. But the real fun in hiking this 70-plus-acre park is crossing all of the sturdy bridges that span the various river channels—built to aid spawning salmon. Kids will absolutely love exploring here.

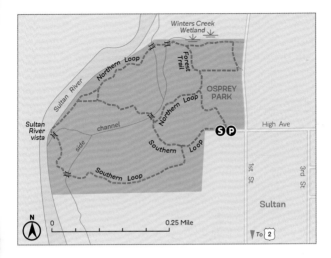

GET MOVING

This park, just north of the small but growing community of Sultan, was once a neglected parcel. But now this slice of riparian forest along the Sultan River is—thanks to many concerned citizens and government officials—a wonderful recreational area and productive wildlife habitat.

Osprey Park's transformation was the result of relicensing the Jackson Hydroelectric Dam upriver, which required that salmon habitat downriver be enhanced. This resulted in the Snohomish County Public Utilities District constructing new channels in the park favoring the spawning fish. This improvement not only makes this parcel excellent wildlife habitat—but also so much fun now to explore. Young explorers will especially enjoy all of the bridges—and all of the loop possibilities. You can easily hike more than 2 miles here. Signage is sparse, so you may get a little confused setting out here for the first time. But half the fun will just be roaming around with no agenda.

At the trailhead just north of the adjacent playfield is a kiosk with a decent map of the park. You can also check out a kiosk displaying a new interpretive map designed by local artist Jacquie Miner. Although this map is a little confusing to use for navigation, it is beautifully illustrated, showing you all of the park's wonderful attributes—wildlife, plant life, and recreation opportunities. The map also pays homage to Bob Knuckey and Susie Hollenbeck, two Sultan residents who recently passed away and had worked tirelessly to improve this park. Two trails within the park are named in honor of these community leaders.

Roam the trails looking for woodpeckers, eagles, kingfishers, thrushes, and yes, ospreys. If you want to witness spawning salmon, you'll need to visit here in autumn. At that time, watch for Chinook, coho, chum, and pink salmon. In spring, look for returning migrating birds setting up nests. Listen to their songs and choruses, in addition to amorous frogs. Enjoy, too, wildflowers adding colorful dabs to the forest floor and nice fragrant touches to the air.

22 Jennings Memorial Park

DISTANCE:	1.5 miles of trails
ELEVATION GAIN:	Minimal
HIGH POINT:	45 feet
DIFFICULTY:	Easy
FITNESS:	Walkers, runners
FAMILY-FRIENDLY:	Yes
DOG-FRIENDLY:	On leash
AMENITIES:	Restrooms, sports fields, Dinosaur Park, picnic tables, gardens, education pavilion
CONTACT/MAPS:	Marysville Parks, Culture and Recreation
GPS:	N 48° 03.587', W 122° 09.692'

GETTING THERE

Driving: From Everett, follow I-5 north for 5 miles to exit 199. Turn right onto State Route 528 (4th Street) and continue for 0.7 mile. Then turn left onto Liberty Street. After 0.1 mile bear right onto Armar Road (Arlington-Marysville Road) and drive 0.4 mile to park and trailhead.

Transit: Community Transit Route 209 stops at the Jennings Nature Park.

Connected to the Jennings Nature Park by a paved trail, Jennings Memorial Park is two parks in one. The two parks comprise 61 acres and contain quite an array of attractions

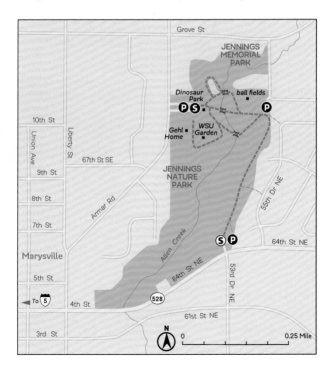

Kid's fishing pond

for their size. And while the trail network is relatively short, count on spending some time here exploring Jennings's historic structures, showy gardens, and wildlife-rich wetlands. Children will particularly like this park—especially its playground, Dinosaur Park.

GET MOVING
Start at the parking area located on a bluff above meandering Allen Creek. Your attention will first be cast upon an old barn, once part of the farm, which was donated to the city by the Jennings family in 1961. The barn is now used as a community

center and recreation hall. Near it is the Gehl home, a 100-plus-year-old house restored by the Marysville Historical Society, open for tours on summer weekends. And behind the home is a 1905 steam donkey (steam-powered winch) in remarkably good shape. After wandering through the historic grounds, check out the nearby Washington State University Master Gardeners Demonstration Site, and if you have a little one with you—set him or her free at Dinosaur Park.

Then do some walking. Follow a wide path off the bluff down toward Allen Creek. The trail passes through a picnic area and then makes a bridged crossing of the creek to playfields and the pavilion. On both sides of the creek, spur trails lead to some spots sure to delight young hikers. The trail near the barn crosses Allen Creek on a floating bridge before traversing a grove of mature conifers. The trail leading left at the picnic grounds circles a kids' fishing pond, crosses Allen Creek, and has branching side trails heading off to patches of skunk cabbage. You can create some short loops by taking these paths.

The main path then bends south at a parking area for the playfields and enters the Jennings Nature Park. The paved path travels over rolling fields and skirts a large wetland. Stately trees line the fields and bluffs encasing the wetland. Several vantage points for observing birds can be accessed by leaving the main path. A spur leads east to 55th Drive NE. The main trail ends at 64th Street NE (SR 528) about 0.6 mile from the main park entrance. Here you'll also find parking, picnic tables, restrooms, and a playground.

GO FARTHER

Off of I-5 exit 206 in Marysville is the Gissberg Twin Lakes County Park. This is a popular spot for taking a walk (or a swim, in season) with 1.1 miles of trails circling the ponds, which were formed by a depression left behind by the construction of I-5. This once was a fairly peaceful spot but is now abutted by big-box stores and strip malls.

23 Arlington Airport Trail

DISTANCE:	5.5 miles roundtrip
ELEVATION GAIN:	50 feet
HIGH POINT:	140 feet
DIFFICULTY:	Easy
FITNESS:	Walkers, runners
FAMILY-FRIENDLY:	Yes, and paved section is jogging stroller– and wheelchair-friendly
DOG-FRIENDLY:	On leash
AMENITIES:	Restrooms, interpretive plaques
CONTACT/MAPS:	City of Arlington Airport Commission; map not available online
GPS:	N 48˚ 09.971', W 122˚ 09.092'

GETTING THERE

Driving: From Everett, head north on I-5 to exit 206. Continue east on State Route 531 (172nd Street NE) for 1.7 miles. Then turn left onto 59th Avenue NE and proceed for 1 mile to airport parking near Bill Quake Memorial Park. The trail can also be accessed from parking areas along Airport Boulevard, 51st Avenue NE, and Bjorn Road.

Transit: Community Transit Routes 220 and 230 stop at the trailhead on 188th Street NE.

Take a run or walk around the periphery of Arlington's historic airport. The trail is mostly soft surface with a short paved section, and it is nearly level for most of its way. While it passes along a fence line and through light business zones, the trail also traverses attractive woods and fields. The views of the surrounding hills are good. And if you're into aviation history (something Snohomish County is noted for)—you'll be flying high here! There are nine interpretive signs along the trail to enlighten you about this little municipal airport's interesting past.

GET MOVING

The Arlington airport was built in 1934 by the Works Progress Administration (WPA) and was used primarily by private fliers and the Forest Service for transporting supplies to fight fires. In 1940 the US Navy leased the airport as an auxiliary air station. The runways were expanded to accommodate bombers during the outbreak of World War II. At one time personnel at the airport included over 700 officers and more than 2200 enlisted men. A third runway was constructed in 1945 along with several warehouses.

After the war, the airport was used primarily as an emergency landing field for Naval Air Station Whidbey. By 1959 it

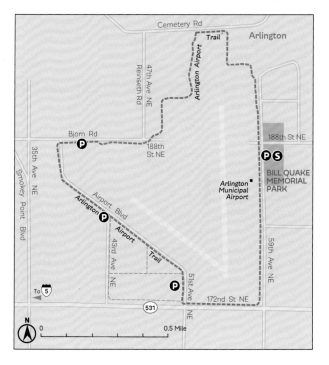

Airport Trail with Mount Pilchuck in the background

was no longer used by the military and became municipal property. It was a popular spot for drag racing during the 1950s and '60s. But the activity was soon banned as the airport became a busier place for private and cargo planes. On your first visit, plan on taking some time along the way at the interpretive signs; they contain a lot of great old photos.

The trail heads around the periphery of the airport, making a 5.5-mile loop, and makes for an excellent running course in its entirety. And because you are in an open area, there are some expansive views of the wooded foothills north and peaks south including Mount Rainier. Expect various aircraft overhead as well.

Although most of the way is level, there are a few dips, particularly along the trail's northern reaches. If you are interested in a short walk on the trail, the best stretches for walking are from the parking areas on Bjorn Road and Airport Boulevard. The trail along Bjorn Road passes through mature fir groves, while the trail parallel to Airport Boulevard is paved, making it ideal for jogging strollers. There are also a couple of spur trails that branch off the loop here: one parallels 43rd Avenue NE, the other cuts through a small patch of forest. They both connect to another trail that can be followed east back to the main loop. These spurs are popular with dog-walkers and allow for some short loops.

GO FARTHER
Just to the north of the airport is the Portage Creek Wildlife Area (accessed from 59th Avenue NE off of SR 531. This 157-acre county reserve (no dogs allowed) consists of about 1.5 miles of trails that traverse open wet meadows (expect winter flooding and flourishing bird life).

24 River Meadows Park

DISTANCE:	6 miles of trails
ELEVATION GAIN:	Up to 150 feet
HIGH POINT:	175 feet
DIFFICULTY:	Easy
FITNESS:	Hikers, runners
FAMILY-FRIENDLY:	Yes
DOG-FRIENDLY:	On leash
AMENITIES:	Restrooms, campground, yurts, picnic shelters
CONTACT/MAPS:	Snohomish County Parks
GPS:	N 48° 10.772', W 122° 05.108'

6.9.18

GETTING THERE
Driving: From Everett, head north on I-5 for 14 miles to exit 208. Then head east on State Route 530 for 4.9 miles, turning

Light snowfall along the South Fork Stillaguamish River

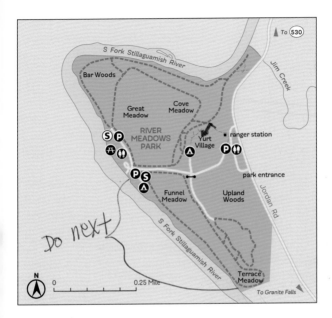

right onto Arlington Heights Road (the turnoff is just after the South Fork Stillaguamish River bridge). Proceed 1 mile, turning right onto Jordan Road. Then continue for 3 more miles to the River Meadows Park entrance. Turn right and follow the park road 0.4 mile to a large parking area near the picnic and camping area by the river.

With **6 miles of trails** traversing woodlots and fallow fields, you can easily spend an entire day wandering through this 150-acre former homestead and farm. And you can easily spend the night here too—and in relative comfort at the park's Yurt Village, located in an old orchard on a terrace above the Great Meadow. The biggest draw to River Meadows, however, is the river: the park fronts 1 mile of the South Fork Stillaguamish River.

2 families

GET MOVING

Throughout most of the year, this park's fields are abuzz with children playing, while the park's riverfront is lined with anglers in waders. The trails, however, never get crowded, and in the winter months they offer plenty of quiet roaming. You can run or hike willy-nilly on the park's trail system, which mostly follows old farm roads, but one of the best routes is the 2.5-mile circuit of the park described below. It touches upon many of the park's attractions and makes for a wonderful introduction to River Meadows Park.

Start your circuit by heading north along the river from the picnic and camping area. Occupying a large bend on the South Fork of the Stillaguamish River, the park offers over 1 mile of river frontage. And while it's been decades since the surrounding meadows have been tilled or grazed, abundant evidence of the park's agrarian past lies scattered throughout the property. These vestiges of simpler times add to the charm of this pastoral park.

The trail travels through a grove of lofty cedars and cottonwoods as it rounds the river bend near a big gravel bar. Marvel at the towering bluffs across the bend. Scan treetops for eagles. Watch the swiftly moving river for mergansers riding the rapids and kingfishers darting into the current. Then continue through a belt of towering trees separating the river from the Great Meadow. The wide trail comes to a junction. The trail to the left continues downstream to Jim Creek. Head right to traverse the Great Meadow, where side trails branch left to the Yurt Village and ranger station. Cross the park access road and follow an old road-turned-trail through the park's Upland Woods. Then descend a small bluff arriving in the Terrace Meadow back along the South Fork Stillaguamish. From here, follow the river once again downstream. Traveling beneath big cedars and along the pretty Funnel Meadow, you'll soon return to the day-use area and your start. You should now be fairly acquainted with the park for future trips and explorations.

Next page: *A hiker on the Bluff Trail above Perego's Lake in Ebey's Landing*

WHIDBEY ISLAND

Washington's largest island is named after Joseph Whidbey, a member of the Royal Navy who served on Captain George Vancouver's expedition to the region in the 1790s. The fourth-largest island in the continental United States (after New York's Long Island, Michigan's Isle Royale, and Texas's Padre Island), Whidbey contains some of the finest beaches within Puget Sound. And thanks to an array of county, state, and national park lands, as well as the active Whidbey Camano Land Trust, the island harbors large tracts of undeveloped land and a large trail network.

Whidbey is home to 60,000 residents, nearly half of whom reside in and around Oak Harbor and its Naval Air Station. Much of the rest of the island is rural. Whidbey Island is about 55 miles long and ranges in width from 1.5 miles to 10 miles—you are never far from the Salish Sea on this landmass. The northern half of the island lies within the Olympic rain shadow and sees some of the lowest annual rainfall amounts within the Puget Basin. However, due to its proximity to the Strait of Juan de Fuca, Whidbey receives its fair share of windstorms. Overall, however, the island's weather is quite agreeable year-round for hiking, walking, and running.

The southern end of the island is connected to the mainland by ferry service to Mukilteo—a short drive from Everett and much of southern Snohomish County. Ferries also connect the island's midsection at Coupeville to Port Townsend on the Olympic Peninsula. And the northern end of the island is connected to the mainland by a series of bridges via Fidalgo Island, allowing for easy access from North Sound communities.

25 Double Bluff

DISTANCE:	4 miles roundtrip
ELEVATION GAIN:	Minimal
HIGH POINT:	10 feet
DIFFICULTY:	Easy
FITNESS:	Walkers, hikers
FAMILY-FRIENDLY:	Yes
DOG-FRIENDLY:	Yes (on and off leash)
AMENITIES:	Restrooms, picnic tables
CONTACT/MAPS:	Island County Parks; map not available online
GPS:	N 47° 58.908', W 122° 30.846'
BEFORE YOU GO:	Very limited parking. If you park on the road, be sure not to block driveways and be well off of right-of-way.

GETTING THERE

Driving from Everett: Drive to the state ferry terminal in Mukilteo and take the ferry to Clinton on Whidbey Island.

Towering bluffs

Then continue north on State Route 525 for 8.5 miles, turning left onto Double Bluff Road (just before milepost 17). Proceed for 2 miles to the road end at Double Bluff County Park and trailhead.

Driving from Oak Harbor: Follow SR 20 south 14.7 miles and continue straight onto SR 525. After 13.3 miles turn right onto Double Bluff Road. Proceed for 2 miles to the road end at Double Bluff County Park and trailhead.

One of the finest beach hikes on the Salish Sea, Double Bluff offers a rare mix of wide sandy shores, stunning Puget Sound scenery, and easy accessibility. A favorite spot among Whidbey Islanders and their dogs, Double Bluff is also perfect for antsy children and anxious city folk needing a good dose of beach walking.

GET MOVING
Although the beaches of Double Bluff can usually be hiked at all tides, low tide is preferable because of the extensive tidal flats that are revealed. The walking is good here on

hardpacked sand—a far cry from the cobbled coastline prevalent throughout the Sound. The 2-mile beach spread before you is public property administered by Island County Parks, Washington State Parks, and the Washington Department of Natural Resources. The towering bluffs and other surrounding uplands, however, are private property, so please respect owners by not trespassing.

Double Bluff has the reputation of being one of the best leash-free dog areas on the Sound. If you do not care to be around scores of free-ranging canines, consider hiking elsewhere. And while the beach is leash-free, the county park where this hike begins requires a leash. So do not let Rover run free until you reach the state-owned tidelands.

Head west along the sandy shoreline cupping Useless Bay. The shallow inlet may not have been much value to ancient mariners, but pelagic and shorebirds find it plenty valuable. Soon approach the first of the towering Double Bluffs. Among the highest coastal bluffs on Puget Sound, they exceed 300 feet in height. But as impressive as they are as a geologic landmark, your attention will be drawn seaward.

Gaze south to Mount Rainier and the Seattle skyline shimmering above the salty horizon. Watch vessels ply Admiralty Inlet. Look east to Mounts Baker, White Chuck, Pilchuck, and Three Fingers. Continue wandering westward and watch a diorama of Olympic peaks unfold before you. At 1.7 miles the beach grows rockier. Here the bluff reveals a conglomerate composition—moraine left behind from the Ice Age glaciers that once shrouded the region. Continue on for another 0.3 mile to round Double Bluff and then call it quits: the tidelands beyond are private. Find a nice rock to perch on. Mutiny Bay lies just to the north, but there's no need to jump ship just yet. Relax and stay for a while, absorbing the splendid coastal scenery surrounding you.

26 Saratoga Woods, Putney Woods, and Metcalf Trust Trails

DISTANCE:	More than 15 miles of trails
ELEVATION GAIN:	Minimal to hundreds of feet
HIGH POINT:	320 feet
DIFFICULTY:	Easy to moderate
FITNESS:	Walkers, hikers, runners, cyclists
FAMILY-FRIENDLY:	Yes, but trails are shared with mountain bikers and horses
DOG-FRIENDLY:	On leash
AMENITIES:	Privy, picnic tables
CONTACT/MAPS:	Island County Parks
GPS:	N 48° 02.672', W 122° 27.775'
BEFORE YOU GO:	Hunting is allowed in the Putney Woods—wear orange in hunting season. Respect all private property postings on adjacent lands.

GETTING THERE

Driving from Everett: Drive to the state ferry terminal in Mukilteo and take the ferry to Clinton on Whidbey Island. Then continue north on State Route 525 for 6.3 miles, turning right onto Bayview Road. Then drive 1.8 miles north, turning left onto E Andreason Road. After 0.6 mile bear right onto Lone Lake Road, then proceed 1.1 miles to the trailhead on your right.

Driving from Oak Harbor: Follow SR 20 south 14.7 miles and continue straight onto SR 525. After 15.6 miles turn left onto Bayview Road. Then drive 1.8 miles north, turning left onto E Andreason Road. After 0.6 mile bear right onto Lone Lake Road, then proceed 1.1 miles to the trailhead on your right.

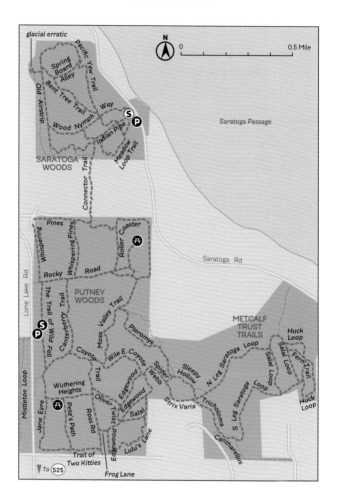

Saratoga, Putney, and Metcalf (sounds like a '60s folk band) comprise more than 15 miles of interconnecting trails. Consisting of more than 800 acres of county parkland and additional private land under public easements, the Saratoga Woods, Putney Woods, and Metcalf Trust trail system make

Whimsical trail name

up the second-largest trail network on Whidbey Island. Take to the system's colorfully named trails and get in a good workout—and perhaps make a discovery or two.

GET MOVING

While the three areas have distinct histories on how they became one big beloved trail system—to most trail users they are one place and usually referred to as just one of the names. The Putney Woods were the former DNR Goss Woods Tract and were renamed for Gary L. Putney, who was instrumental in developing the extensive trail system here. The Metcalf Trust Trails are on land for which the Metcalf family granted a public recreation easement. And the Saratoga Woods were protected by a group of citizens, along with the Whidbey Camano Land Trust, and added to the system.

In general, the Putney Woods tract contains young scrappy forest, because much of this area was logged in the 1980s. The Metcalf Trust Trails contain both recently logged and mature second-growth. The Saratoga Woods offer the most diversity, with older forest and old pastures. The Saratoga Woods also offer more landscape diversity, with steeper slopes, a broad hilltop once used as an airstrip, and a massive glacial erratic—one of the largest in the state. The Saratoga and Metcalf trails traverse fairly level ground, but there are some dips and small hollows here and there to give you a little elevation gain on longer walks and runs.

The trail system here is pretty complex. It's fairly well marked within the Saratoga Woods and Metcalf Trust properties. But you should definitely print or download a map before heading out—or you will have a difficult time trying to figure out where you are and may end up unintentionally extending your workout. Note that at the eastern end of the trail system navigation can get a little confusing. Here the Huck Loop passes through a fairly recent clear-cut. The trail isn't well defined and it is easy to end up on a skid road leading off of the trust trails.

While much of the terrain is fairly uniform, the trail names add a lot of color. Pteromys, Jane Eyre, Trail of Two Kitties, and Tricholoma are sure to pique your interest. There are several access points to these trails, but many originate from private property or areas without parking. The two trailheads with parking include the one listed in the info block (on Lone Lake Road) and one for Saratoga Woods from Saratoga Road, approximately 3 miles west of Langley.

A grand circuit around the Putney and Metcalf woods is about 5.5 miles. Add the connector to Saratoga and make a circuit there and you are now looking at more than 8 miles. There are even more trails on the west side of Lone Lake Road. You can easily spend a day hiking here or getting in an ultrarunning workout.

27 South Whidbey State Park

DISTANCE:	4 miles of trails
ELEVATION GAIN:	Up to 350 feet
HIGH POINT:	425 feet

DIFFICULTY:	Easy to moderate
FITNESS:	Hikers
FAMILY-FRIENDLY:	Yes
DOG-FRIENDLY:	On leash
AMENITIES:	Privy, picnic shelters, water, benches, interpretive signs, pay phone
CONTACT/MAPS:	Washington State Parks
GPS:	N 48˚ 03.370', W 122˚ 35.445'
BEFORE YOU GO:	Discover Pass required.

GETTING THERE

Driving from Everett: Drive to the state ferry terminal in Mukilteo and take the ferry to Clinton on Whidbey Island. Then continue north on State Route 525 for 10.5 miles, turning left onto Bush Point Road. After 2.2 miles the road becomes Smugglers Cove Road. Continue for another 2.7 miles to the trailhead on your left at the state park day-use parking area.

Driving from Oak Harbor: Follow SR 20 south 14.7 miles and continue straight onto SR 525. After 4.7 miles turn right onto Smugglers Cove Road and continue 4.3 miles to trailhead on your right at the state park day-use parking area.

Transit: Island Transit Route 56

The beach is grand, but South Whidbey State Park's best attribute is its forest: it's over 250 years old and is home to massive cedars and Douglas firs. One of the finest tracts of old-growth remaining on Whidbey Island, it was nearly logged in the 1970s. Today, a trail bearing the name of the husband and wife responsible for mobilizing the public to protect it weaves through the impressive grove. A handful of other trails traverse this pretty park, too, leading to scenic views and quiet woodlands.

GET MOVING

There are several trails in this 347-acre state park. For a warm-up, head east on the short 0.3-mile Forest Discovery South Loop. This trail leads down to a small ravine, crossing

Old-growth forest

a cascading creek twice and offering some blufftop window views to Marrowstone Island across Admiralty Inlet. When finished with this loop, continue on the rest of the Forest Discovery Trail to the state park's picnic area and then walk through the now closed (due to the risk of falling diseased trees) campground. Here you can hike the short Hobbit Trail to a bluff above the beach—or to the beach itself on the Beach Trail. Note, however, that the Beach Trail might be closed due to erosion (respect any closures). If the trail is open, you will have nearly a mile of public shoreline to explore.

The hiking highlight here, however, is the old-growth forest located across the road. From the day-use parking area, carefully cross Smugglers Cove Road and locate the trailhead for the Ridge Loop Trail. Start up the trail and immediately come to a junction at a big Sitka spruce. The trail to

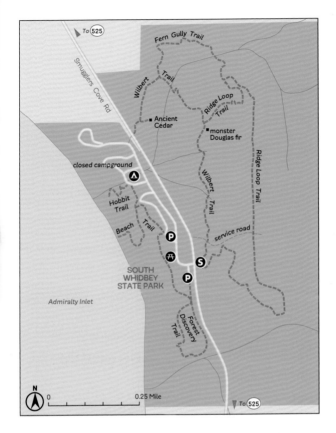

To (525)

Fern Gully Trail

Smugglers Cove Rd

Wilbert Trail

Ridge Loop Trail

Ancient Cedar

monster Douglas fir

Ridge Loop Trail

closed campground

Hobbit Trail

Wilbert Trail

Beach Trail

service road

SOUTH WHIDBEY STATE PARK

Admiralty Inlet

Forest Discovery Trail

N

0   0.25 Mile

To (525)

the left is the Wilbert Trail. This trail is named for tree huggers (literally) Meryl and Harry Wilbert: they, along with several others, helped preserve the ancient forest here.

You can combine the 0.8-mile Wilbert Trail with the Ridge Loop and Fern Gully trails for a 2.3-mile loop. It makes a great hike. To do this loop, head right on the Ridge Loop Trail and gradually climb, passing some big firs. The way winds east under a lush canopy and through thickets of evergreen huckleberries and big boughs of ferns. After traversing an alder grove, the trail swings west utilizing an old Department of Natural Resources road. With your elevation gain now complete, enjoy easy walking. Intersect another old road (which can be followed left for a short loop back to the Wilbert Trail) and continue straight, eventually coming to a junction.

The Ridge Loop heads left. You want to go right on the Fern Gully Trail, descending into a dark draw of massive firs and spruces. After crossing a wet flat, intersect the Wilbert Trail. But before returning left, head right for a short distance to the "Ancient Cedar," a lone behemoth five centuries old. Read the plaque about the Wilberts, whose "tree hugging" led to the preservation of this cedar and 255 acres of surrounding forest.

Then return right on the Wilbert Trail, passing junctions with the Fern Gully and Ridge Loop trails and continuing through breathtakingly beautiful groves of ancient cedars and spruces. After a small climb, come to a monster Douglas fir, quite possibly the biggest tree on Whidbey Island. Continue a short distance to return to the trailhead.

28 Trillium Community Forest

DISTANCE:	7 miles of trails
ELEVATION GAIN:	Up to 300 feet
HIGH POINT:	425 feet
DIFFICULTY:	Easy to moderate
FITNESS:	Hikers, runners, cyclists
FAMILY-FRIENDLY:	Yes, but trails shared with mountain bikes and equestrians
DOG-FRIENDLY:	On leash
AMENITIES:	None
CONTACT/MAPS:	Whidbey Camano Land Trust
GPS:	N 48˚ 02.546', W 122˚ 35.405'
BEFORE YOU GO:	Hunting is allowed in season; wear orange.

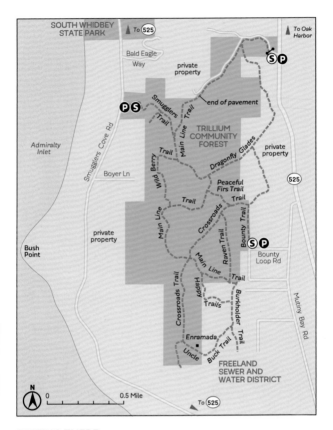

GETTING THERE

Driving from Everett: Drive to the state ferry terminal in Mukilteo and take the ferry to Clinton on Whidbey Island. Then continue north on State Route 525 for 10.5 miles, turning left onto Bush Point Road. After 2.2 miles the road becomes Smugglers Cove Road. Continue for another 1.7 miles to the large parking area and trailhead on your right.

Driving from Oak Harbor: Follow SR 20 south 14.7 miles and continue straight onto SR 525. After 4.7 miles turn right

Filtered sunlight at Trillium Community Forest

onto Smugglers Cove Road and continue 5.3 miles to the large parking area and trailhead on your left.

Transit: Island Transit Route 56

Thank the Great Recession for this 700-plus-acre tract of protected forest—one of the largest undeveloped parcels on the island. This area was slated for high-density housing, but the developer went bankrupt, and the Whidbey Camano Land Trust led a fundraising drive in order to buy it. Fifteen hundred folks pitched in to create this community forest, now containing 7 miles of trails (many old skid roads) perfect for easy strolls and long runs.

GET MOVING

Originally logged several times before being sold to an invest-ment developer, the Trillium Community Forest is no pristine tract of woods. But forests grow back (if not developed) and habitat can be restored. The Whidbey Camano Land Trust saw the value (beyond housing tracts) in this large piece of real estate—mainly to protect watersheds and provide wildlife habitat as well as a place for passive recreation. Most of the forest is fairly young here, but that will change over the years.

There is no *wow* factor here as far as the landscape goes, but you have 7 miles of well-marked, uncrowded trails to hike, walk, and run. The trails are open to mountain bikes and equestrians too. Note that several trails lead out of the for-est to adjacent horse farms and homes—respect all private property. Note too that several trails on the forest's eastern edge traverse Freeland Sewer and Water District property and private property—but easements have been granted for these trails. Stay on the trail and respect any closures or postings. Also, be aware that the community forest is open to the public—but is privately owned (by the land trust)—so respect all rules and keep your dog leashed (or risk having them banned).

From the trailhead follow the Smugglers Trail into an attractive forest grove and climb up a small ridge. Soon cross into younger forest (the demarcation quite pronounced), pass a short spur on your right, and reach a junction with the Main Line (an old skid road) at 0.5 mile. From here you have several options for short and long loops. The terrain is pretty level with some elevation loss toward the forest's southern end. Note that the Main Line heading left eventually becomes a paved road. It is gated and open for a handful of homeowners on the forest's northern periphery to access their properties. This direction will also lead you to a developed trailhead at the road gate—an alternative starting point and easily reached from SR 525. For a short loop of about 2.5 miles, follow the Main Line right to the Dragonfly Glades, then back to the Main Line, and then right to the Smugglers Trail.

For a much longer loop of about 5.7 miles that travels much of the forest's northern periphery, head right down the Main Line Trail to the Crossroads Trail. Go right on this trail, taking a left on Uncle Buck and passing through an outdoor worship area known as the Enramada. Take a left on the Burkholder Trail back to the Main Line. Go left and then immediately take a right on the Raven Trail. Follow the Crossroads right to the Dragonfly Glades. You'll pass the Bounty Trail, which leads south 0.3 mile to another developed trailhead (on the Bounty Loop Road) for an alternative start. This trailhead is ADA-accessible and also provides access to a short ADA accessible loop trail. To finish the long loop, go right on the Dragonfly Glades, then left on the Main Line back to the Smugglers Trail. You can also extend this loop by hitting some of those connecting trails you passed by.

Have fun creating your own workout and exploration loops in this sprawling area. Trail advocates are hoping to someday connect Trillium Community Forest to South Whidbey State Park.

29 Greenbank Farm

DISTANCE:	More than 4 miles of trails
ELEVATION GAIN:	Up to 280 feet
HIGH POINT:	300 feet
DIFFICULTY:	Easy
FITNESS:	Walkers, hikers, runners
FAMILY-FRIENDLY:	Yes; forest trails open to horses
DOG-FRIENDLY:	Yes, off leash
AMENITIES:	Restrooms, benches, art, café and shops, Whidbey Camano Land Trust office
CONTACT/MAPS:	Port of Coupeville
GPS:	N 48˚ 06.453', W 122˚ 34.507'
BEFORE YOU GO:	Greenbank is an off-leash park. If you're not fond of roving Rovers, it's best to hike elsewhere.

GETTING THERE

Driving from Everett: Drive to the state ferry terminal in Mukilteo and take the ferry to Clinton on Whidbey Island. Then continue north on State Route 525 for 17 miles, passing through the small community of Greenbank and turning right onto Wonn Road. Proceed for 0.2 mile, turning left into the large parking area for Greenbank Farm and trailhead.

Driving from Oak Harbor: Follow SR 20 south 14.7 miles and continue straight onto SR 525. After 4.8 miles turn left onto Wonn Road. Proceed for 0.2 mile, turning left into the large parking area for Greenbank Farm and trailhead.

Transit: Island Transit Route 56 stops at the nearby Greenbank Park and Ride.

This historic farm was once destined to become a 700-home self-contained community. But, thanks to the rallying of local residents, it's now a living history farm, cultural

Young hiker at Greenbank Farm

community center, and scenic and recreational gem. Straddling the narrowest point on Whidbey Island, numerous trails traverse the fielded and forested sprawling farm. From Greenbank's rolling pastures, feast your eyes on inspiring maritime and mountain views.

GET MOVING
From dairying to the largest loganberry farm in the United States, Greenbank has had a productive and flavorful history on Washington's largest island. But in the 1990s wine producers at Chateau Ste. Michelle wanted to turn this scenic and serene piece of our agricultural heritage into a sprawling suburban housing tract. *Mon Dieu!* What were they thinking?!

Luckily for those of us who believe that farmland is better off unpaved, a large consortium of local citizens convinced the

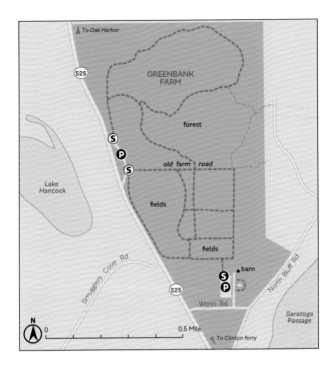

vintner to negotiate with the Trust for Public Land instead, which had far nobler intentions for this 522-acre tract of rural beauty. The Trust for Public Land in turn sold the land to Island County, the Port of Coupeville, and The Nature Conservancy to be preserved and managed as a living history farm for all to enjoy.

Dog owners in particular enjoy Greenbank Farm. If well-behaved and non-aggressive, Rover and company are allowed to roam the premises (away from the farm buildings) unfettered from their leashes. Children will be fond of Greenbank's horses, farm buildings, old farm equipment, and the small farm pond usually hosting ducks and geese.

The southern half of the farm consists of rolling pasture. Several trails traverse the open expanse and they all make for fine ambling. The center trail, however, follows along a ridge crest granting the best views. Gallivant for a half mile across the grassy ridge, grazing on views east across Saratoga Passage to Camano Island, Three Fingers, and Mount Pilchuck, and west to wildlife-rich Lake Hancock (closed to public access) and across Admiralty Inlet to the craggy eastern front of the Olympic Mountains. A walk around the meadow's periphery will yield at least 1.5 miles on your fitness tracker.

A blackberry-lined trail (an old farm road) runs along the field's northern edge. If you follow it west, it leads to an alternative trailhead (located on SR 525). About midway along this trail locate a signed fencepost marking the beginning of the farm's forest trails. You can continue north here, gently climbing through a forest of hemlock and fir. The trail winds through thickets of waxy leaf salal, evergreen huckleberries, and rhododendrons on good tread. After about 0.4 mile it comes to a junction. Go in either direction for a pleasant mile-or-so loop through quiet forest. A short trail branches off of the loop leading to the alternative trailhead, from where you can follow the trail along the field's edge back to the signpost. Then choose your path (they're all good) back to the trailhead at the farm.

30 Fort Casey Historical State Park

DISTANCE:	1.8 miles of trails and more than 2 miles of coastal beach
ELEVATION GAIN:	Up to 90 feet
HIGH POINT:	90 feet
DIFFICULTY:	Easy
FITNESS:	Walkers, hikers
FAMILY-FRIENDLY:	Yes
DOG-FRIENDLY:	On leash

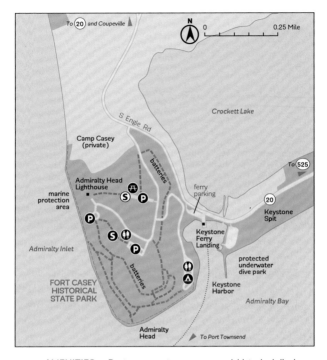

AMENITIES: Restrooms, water, campground, historical displays, old fort, lighthouse, picnic tables
CONTACT/MAPS: Washington State Parks
GPS: N 48° 09.510', W 122° 40.715'
BEFORE YOU GO: Discover Pass required.

GETTING THERE

Driving from Everett: Drive to the state ferry terminal in Mukilteo and take the ferry to Clinton on Whidbey Island. Then continue north on State Route 525 for 22 miles. Turn left onto SR 20 and proceed for 3.4 miles, passing the Coupeville-Keystone Ferry. Now on S Engle Road, continue for 0.4 mile. Then turn left, entering Fort Casey Historical State Park, and drive 0.5 mile to the large parking area and trailhead.

Bluff top trail at Fort Casey

Driving from Oak Harbor: Follow SR 20 south 9.5 miles to the traffic light in Coupeville. Turn right onto S Main Street (which becomes S Engle Road) and continue for 3.6 miles. Then turn right, entering Fort Casey Historical Park, and drive 0.5 mile to the large parking area and trailhead.

Transit: Island Transit Route 6

If ever there was a park perfect for dilly-dallying, this is the one. With its lighthouse—an iconic sight on Whidbey Island—and its extensive fort, complete with bunkers and batteries, Fort Casey Historical State Park calls out to be explored in a leisurely fashion. Beyond the ramparts, quiet trails traverse the maritime forest and flowered meadows grace Admiralty Head. And the park contains more than 2 miles of windswept coastline begging to be walked as well.

GET MOVING

Occupying the small headland of Admiralty Head on the east side of Admiralty Inlet, Fort Casey was once part of the national defense system protecting the country's coasts and waterways. Along with Fort Flagler on Marrowstone Island and Fort Worden on the Quimper Peninsula, Fort Casey was part of the "Triangle of Fire" designed to protect the entrance to Puget Sound. First constructed in the 1890s and once containing state-of-the-art technology, after World War II the fort became obsolete.

Many of the fortifications were acquired by Washington State Parks, while the former barracks and officers' housing now known as the Camp Casey Conference Center were acquired by Seattle Pacific University (SPU). In the late 1980s the adjacent Keystone Spit was added to the state park. This magnificent stretch of coastline was threatened with ill-conceived housing developments, but thanks to dedicated conservationists and enlightened public officials (yes, they do exist), it was protected.

Begin exploring at the large day-use parking area. Just to the north is the elegant Admiralty Head Lighthouse, built in 1903. It houses historical displays and is regularly open to the public (check park website for hours). You are free to roam west and south, too, exploring the fort's batteries. Have fun walking through, on, and around them—but keep children close by, as there aren't many railings and a fall could be less than pretty.

East of the parking area a couple of trails traverse woods and lead to the picnic area. From here you can cross the park road and take another trail past two of the quieter batteries and work your way back to the main installation. Be sure to also explore the trails leading off the bluffs and to the shoreline. Try to plan for a low tide and enjoy some serious surf strolling. You can walk the tidelands north of the park (actually part of the Pacific Northwest Trail; see "Pacific Northwest Trail" sidebar) to Ebey's Landing National Historical Reserve (see Trail 32). But note that the uplands are private property. Camp Casey is closed to unregistered visitors and a half-mile stretch of coastline to the north is private property, through

PACIFIC NORTHWEST TRAIL

Back during the backpacking boom of the 1970s, transplanted New Englander Ron Strickland was struck with a novel idea. How about adding another classic long-distance hiking trail to our country's stock—one to accompany and rival the likes of the Appalachian and Pacific Crest trails? Such began his quest to build the Pacific Northwest Trail (PNT), a 1200-mile path from Cape Alava on the Olympic Peninsula to Montana's Glacier National Park.

Soon forming the Pacific Northwest Trail Association, Strickland and a slew of tireless volunteers set out to promote, construct, and maintain the new trail. Utilizing existing trails along with new tread, the PNT travels through Whidbey Island on its way from the Pacific to the Rockies. While parts of the trail still follow roads, much progress is being made on completing the PNT since President Barack Obama signed a bill in 2009 designating it a national scenic trail—a status that the PCT and AT also both hold.

You can hike or run along portions of the PNT in the following trails in this book: Fort Casey Historical State Park (see Trail 30); Ebey's Landing National Historical Reserve (see Trail 32); Fort Ebey State Park (see Trail 33); Joseph Whidbey State Park (see Trail 35); Goose Rock and Cranberry Lake at Deception Pass State Park (see Trail 38); and Hoypus Point Natural Forest Area at Deception Pass State Park (see Trail 39). Visit www.pnt.org for more information.

which public access can be revoked at any time—so heed all postings and rules.

There is additional public shoreline at the Keystone Spit, a part of the state park but separated from the main section by the Washington State Ferry dock. You can walk along S Engle Road to reach it—or drive to a couple of parking lots there. There are restrooms at the spit in the state park and the adjacent Driftwood County Park. Enjoy more than 1.5 miles of uncrowded beach walking. On the spit's north side is Crockett Lake, a large estuarine lake that offers some of the best bird-watching on Whidbey Island. If you decide to check it out, please tread lightly and give all wildlife plenty of space.

Admiralty Inlet Preserve

31

DISTANCE:	2.3 miles of trails
ELEVATION GAIN:	Up to 125 feet
HIGH POINT:	175 feet
DIFFICULTY:	Easy
FITNESS:	Walkers, hikers
FAMILY-FRIENDLY:	Yes
DOG-FRIENDLY:	On leash
AMENITIES:	Interpretive signs, benches
CONTACT/MAPS:	Whidbey Camano Land Trust
GPS:	N 48˚ 10.698', W 122˚ 41.217'

GETTING THERE

Driving from Everett: Drive to the state ferry terminal in Mukilteo and take the ferry to Clinton on Whidbey Island. Then continue north on State Route 525 for 22 miles. Turn left onto SR 20 and proceed for 3.4 miles, passing the Coupeville-Keystone Ferry. Now on S Engle Road, continue for 1.5 miles to the trailhead on your left.

Driving from Oak Harbor: Follow SR 20 south 9.5 miles to the traffic light in Coupeville. Turn right onto S Main Street (which becomes S Engle Road) and continue for 2.5 miles to the trailhead on your right.

Transit: Island Transit Route 6

Occupying a lofty coastal bluff just north of Fort Casey Historical State Park, this new Whidbey Camano Land Trust preserve is full of historical and scenic surprises. Explore the remains of a military fire control station. Savor stunning views across Admiralty Inlet to the Quimper Peninsula and Olympic Mountains. Marvel at a forest of ancient, contorted trees. And if you visit in the spring, delight in a dazzling display of prairie flowers—some quite rare.

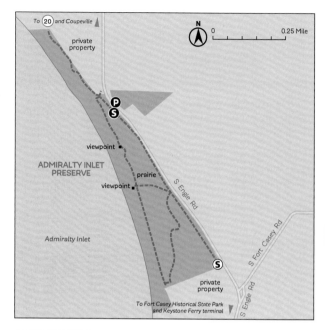

GET MOVING

This property was once part of the Fort Casey military installation, built to protect Puget Sound from enemy attack. The fort eventually became obsolete and this part of the installation became part of Seattle Pacific University's Camp Casey Conference Center. Recognizing the ecological importance of this property, the Whidbey Camano Land Trust purchased it from the university in 2013.

The preserve, now at 79 acres, contains a rare prairie habitat supporting golden paintbrush, a showy flower that exists in the wild in just a handful of places worldwide. The trust is currently restoring the prairie to a more natural state by eradicating invasive species. Please stay on the trails, respect all closures, and keep your dog leashed. Also, because this preserve is a place for wildlife and nature observation, all of

Old-growth forest at the preserve

the trails except for the 0.7-mile one paralleling S Engle Road are closed to running.

There are 2.3 miles of trails in the preserve. Weave together a couple of loops and short out-and-backs to easily hike through the entire property. Although it's fairly small, the preserve contains incredible diversity. The southern half of the preserve is home to a forest more than 250 years old. Here on a high coastal bluff subjected to constant storms, the trees are much shorter than their mountain valley counterparts of equal age. While their size may not be remarkable, their contorted shapes are, thanks to constantly being bombarded by strong winds.

You can walk along the edge of the 175-foot bluff for 1.1 miles enjoying stunted trees, fort remains, and spectacular views across Admiralty Inlet. Sunsets are superb along this trail. There are a lot of interpretive signs to help you appreciate all of the natural beauty and history around you. And although Fort Casey Historical State Park is nearby, unless you are a guest at the Camp Casey Conference Center, do not use the trails on this private property to reach the park.

32 Ebey's Landing National Historical Reserve

DISTANCE:	5.2 miles
ELEVATION GAIN:	310 feet
HIGH POINT:	260 feet
DIFFICULTY:	Moderate
FITNESS:	Hikers
FAMILY-FRIENDLY:	Yes
DOG-FRIENDLY:	On leash
AMENITIES:	Restrooms, interpretive signs, historic sites, picnic tables
CONTACT/MAPS:	Ebey's Landing National Historical Reserve
GPS:	N 48˚ 12.296', W 122˚ 42.369'

GETTING THERE

Driving from Everett: Drive to the state ferry terminal in Mukilteo and take the ferry to Clinton on Whidbey Island.

A hiker on the Bluff Trail above Perego's Lake in Ebey's Landing

Then continue north on State Route 525 for 22 miles and proceed straight on SR 20. Drive for 6.3 miles on SR 20 and turn left onto S Sherman Road (the turnoff is 0.8 mile north of the Coupeville traffic light). Then proceed for 0.3 mile, turning right onto Cook Road. After another 0.3 mile reach the Prairie Overlook and trailhead.

Driving from Oak Harbor: Follow SR 20 south 8.7 miles and turn right onto S Sherman Road. Then proceed for 0.3 mile, turning right onto Cook Road. After another 0.3 mile reach the Prairie Overlook and trailhead.

Transit: Island Transit Route 6 stops near the Kettles Spur Trail.

Stroll across emerald fields, climb coastal bluffs towering above crashing surf, and wander along a driftwood log–strewn beach, gazing across busy coastal waters to a backdrop of snowcapped Olympic Mountains. And there's more! With prairie flowers, bald eagles, shorebirds, and historic relics, Ebey's Landing is one of Washington's most naturally diverse and historically significant places.

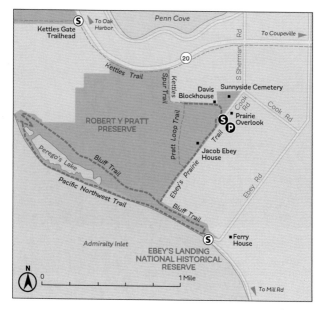

GET MOVING

Brimming with history as well as natural beauty, Ebey's Landing National Historical Reserve encompasses a mélange of protected lands (see "Ebey's Landing National Historical Reserve" sidebar in Trail 33). It also contains miles of trails. The prairie-bluff-shore lollipop loop described here is a classic Washington hike. Starting from near the Prairie Overlook, head west on the Ebey's Prairie Trail. The Pratt Loop Trail veers right and offers an extended hike (see Go Farther).

At 0.3 mile come to the restored 1850s Jacob Ebey House (Jacob Ebey was the father of Issac, whom the reserve is named for), which now serves as a visitor center (open seasonally). Be sure to check out the adjacent blockhouse, one of four in the reserve. Then continue hiking west toward the sea across an emerald lawn reminiscent of Ireland. Pass the western end of the Pratt Loop Trail and at 0.8 mile reach a junction

EBEY'S LANDING NATIONAL HISTORICAL RESERVE

Ebey's Landing National Historical Reserve was named for Colonel Isaac Neff Ebey, who in the 1850s became one of Whidbey Island's first non-Native settlers. The blockhouse he erected to defend his land claim from Native attacks still stands, watching over prairies that have been in continual agricultural use for over 160 years. Prominent in territorial affairs, Ebey was slain in 1857 by a band of Haidas seeking revenge for the killing of one of their own chieftains by settlers.

The blockhouse, prairies, and much of the surrounding land are now protected within the Ebey's Landing National Historical Reserve, a special unit of the National Park Service (NPS). Created in 1978, Ebey's Landing differs from other park units in that most of the lands within it remain in private ownership and are managed through partnerships and overseen by a trust consisting of representatives from state, county, and local governments, the NPS, and the local community. While the NPS does own several parcels within the reserve, as do Washington State Parks and The Nature Conservancy, the majority of the land remains privately owned. On many of these lands the NPS has purchased development rights, assuring that the lands maintain their historic and scenic integrity. More than 5500 acres of the reserve's 17,572 acres are still being used for agriculture, as they have been since pioneers settled here.

Note that National Park Service land within the reserve requires no fee to visit. However, state parks within the reserve require a Discover Pass. Private land within the reserve (without public easements) is private property and should not be trespassed upon.

with the Bluff Trail. This is a lollipop loop. You'll be returning on the left. Head right, climbing golden coastal bluffs lined with contorted firs and bursting with blossoms in the spring. Reaching heights of 260 feet, these are among the highest coastal bluffs in Puget Sound.

Gaze out to the snowcapped Olympics, the Strait of Juan de Fuca, Vancouver Island, and the San Juan Islands. Watch ferries and ocean vessels ply busy Admiralty Inlet. Look for majestic bald eagles perched in ghostly snags. Notice prickly pear cactus growing on the sun-kissed slopes. Stare straight down at Perego's Lake, a shorebird-harboring lagoon formed by a narrow spit and littered with giant drift logs.

Walk along the bluff crest for a good mile, coming to a junction with a short spur trail heading to an excellent viewpoint. Then steeply descend, coming to the trail's end at a wide beach of hardpacked sand and polished stones. Turn left and walk south along the beach, rounding the spit and reaching the Ebey's Landing Wayside within Ebey's Landing State Park (alternative start, Discover Pass required) at 4 miles. Pick up the Bluff Trail once again and climb stairs back up a coastal bluff. Reach a familiar junction at 4.4 miles. Turn right and hike 0.8 mile back to your starting point.

GO FARTHER

You can hike the beach north 2.2 miles to Fort Ebey State Park (see Trail 33) or south 2.5 miles to Fort Casey Historical State Park (see Trail 30). You can also extend your hike on the uplands. Follow the fairly new Pratt Loop Trail around pasture and along the Pratt Woods (a Nature Conservancy preserve). This 1.3-mile loop also leads to old farm structures. And you can extend your hike even more by taking the Kettles Spur Trail, which branches off the Pratt Loop Trail in 0.75 mile, connecting to the Kettles Trail (see Trail 34).

33 Fort Ebey State Park

DISTANCE:	More than 30 miles of trails
ELEVATION GAIN:	Up to hundreds of feet
HIGH POINT:	210 feet
DIFFICULTY:	Easy to moderate
FITNESS:	Walkers, hikers, runners, cyclists
FAMILY-FRIENDLY:	Yes, but note many trails open to equestrians and mountain bikes

View from the Bluff Trail

DOG-FRIENDLY:	On leash
AMENITIES:	Restrooms, campground, picnic area, interpretive trails, park store, historic exhibits and features, paraglider launch area
CONTACT/MAPS:	Washington State Parks
GPS:	N 48° 13.147', W 122° 45.744'
BEFORE YOU GO:	Discover Pass required; park open from 8:00 AM to dusk.

GETTING THERE

Driving from Everett: Drive to Mukilteo and take the Washington State Ferry to Clinton on Whidbey Island. Drive State Route 525 north for 22 miles, then continue straight on SR 20 for 8.9 miles (passing through Coupeville) and turn left onto Libbey Road. Proceed for 0.9 mile and turn left onto Hill Valley

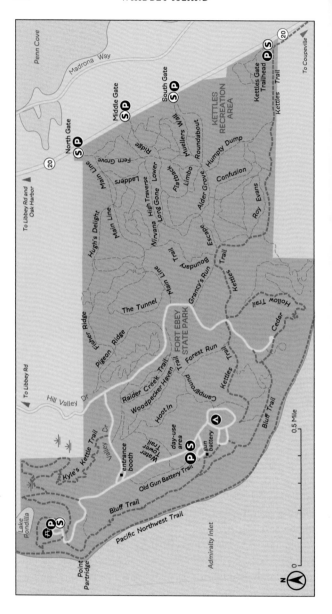

Drive. After 0.7 mile, bear right onto Valley Drive and continue 0.3 mile, passing through the state park entrance booth, to a junction. Then head left 0.4 mile and turn right, reaching the trailhead and parking at a gun battery.

Driving from Oak Harbor: Drive south on SR 20 for 6 miles and turn right onto Libbey Road. Proceed for 0.9 mile and turn left onto Hill Valley Drive. After 0.7 mile, bear right onto Valley Drive and continue 0.3 mile, passing through the state park entrance booth, to a junction. Then head left 0.4 mile and turn right, reaching the trailhead and parking at a gun battery.

Transit: Island Transit Route 6 stops at the county park trailhead on SR 20.

The last fort to be built as part of the Puget Sound harbor defense system, Fort Ebey now protects more than 3 miles of stunning Salish Sea coastline. Fort Ebey also contains a fine campground and, along with the abutting Kettles Recreation Area, contains more than 30 miles of trail on nearly 900 acres of public property. With the largest trail network on the island, you can spend many days here hiking or running the towering coastal bluffs, a wild windswept shoreline, and a pockmarked, forested landscape known as the Kettles. **Note:** Horses share the trails on the Island County–owned Kettles Recreation Area and hunting is permitted in season here.

GET MOVING

Unlike the nearby forts of Casey, Worden, and Flagler, which made up the "Triangle of Fire" and date back to the 1890s, Fort Ebey wasn't constructed until World War II. Equipped with the newest technology at the time, it soon became obsolete and was decommissioned shortly after the war. The state purchased the fort site in the 1960s for a state park, and through subsequent purchases, including a large tract of adjacent Department of Natural Resources land, the park grew to its current size of more than 600 acres.

The best hikes in the park include the nearly 2 miles of spectacular coastline beneath towering bluffs—and the hiker-only Bluff Trail, which follows atop those lofty coastal bluffs. The Bluff Trail passes by viewpoints, the Point Partridge beacon, an old fort gun battery, as well as a popular paragliding spot. There is no way to make a loop out of the bluff and shore, so you'll need to do an out-and-back on the shoreline, which also currently serves as the Pacific Northwest Trail route through the park. You can, however, make several loops and extensions from the Bluff Trail.

Consider the trail to Lake Pondilla, a small kettle pond. And near the lake is the Kyle's Kettle Trail, which is a quiet hiker-only path that traverses patches of rhododendrons. Almost all of the park's other trails, as well as the ones in the adjacent county lands, are also open to mountain bikes. The county trails are open to horses as well. Most of these interconnecting trails traverse a uniform landscape of young evergreen forest interspersed with madrones, rhododendron, and other shrubs and deciduous trees. The trails wind down, around, up, and through a series of kettles—deep hollows left behind by receding Ice Age glaciers.

These kettle trails are very popular with mountain bikers and trail runners. Some are old logging roads, others are narrow single-track through brushy undergrowth and dark forest. Hikers can certainly take them, but probably won't find many of them too interesting. The Cedar Hollow Trail, however, is an interesting path plummeting into and then climbing out of a deep forested gap in the coastal bluffs. The long-distance Kettles Trail (see Trail 34) starts in the park's campground and travels east for about 1.7 miles, first as single-track, then as old road, before reaching the Kettles Gate Trailhead on SR 20 and becoming a paved path. In general, if you are looking for an area to put some serious trail mileage in—the trail system here at Fort Ebey will satisfy you.

34 **Kettles Trail**

DISTANCE:	3.6 miles one-way
ELEVATION GAIN:	160 feet
HIGH POINT:	210 feet
DIFFICULTY:	Easy
FITNESS:	Walkers, runners, cyclists
FAMILY-FRIENDLY:	Yes, and jogging stroller– and wheelchair-friendly
DOG-FRIENDLY:	On leash
AMENITIES:	Benches, restrooms, picnic tables, and campground in Rhododendron County Park
CONTACT/MAPS:	Island County Parks
GPS:	N 48° 12.487', W 122° 39.267'

GETTING THERE

Driving from Everett: Drive to Mukilteo and take the Washington State Ferry to Clinton on Whidbey Island. Then drive SR 525 north for 22 miles. Continue straight on State Route 20 for 3.9 miles and turn left onto Park Road. Continue 0.1 mile into Rhododendron County Park and park near the campground gate for the trailhead.

Driving from Oak Harbor: Drive south on SR 20 for 11 miles and turn right (turnoff is 1.8 miles beyond the Coupeville traffic light) onto Park Road. Continue 0.1 mile into Rhododendron County Park and park near the campground gate for the trailhead.

Transit: Island Transit Routes 1NB and 1SB stop at the Coupeville Park and Ride near the trail crossing at S Main Street.

Run or walk this paved path through pasture and prairie in the heart of Ebey's Landing National Historical Reserve. Although this trail parallels SR 20, don't let that discourage you. The views across the rolling rural landscape to the Olympic

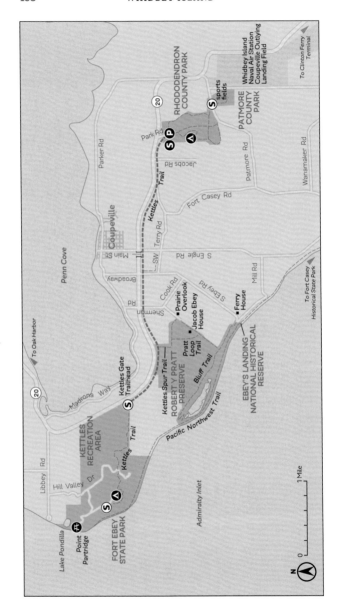

Mountains and Cascades are stunning. In season, the flowers are divine as are the flocks of songbirds—none of which can be enjoyed buzzing along the highway at 50 miles per hour.

GET MOVING

The Kettles Trail (sometimes referred to as the Rhododendron Trail east of Coupeville's Main Street) is a paved path that connects Island County's Rhododendron County Park with the Kettles Recreation Area. This paved route offers a safe 3.6-mile, off-highway passage for area bicyclists. But it also makes for a good running and walking path. The only downside can be the nearby highway noise—but it's nothing a pair of earbuds can't address.

The Kettles Trail actually continues beyond its western paved terminus as a soft-surface trail to Fort Ebey State Park (see Trail 33). And from its eastern terminus it connects to a network of trails in Rhododendron County Park, allowing for extended wanderings (see Go Farther, below). You can also park and begin at Rhododendron County Park's sports fields on Patmore Road, the Kettles Gate Trailhead on SR 20, or at the gun battery day-use area in Fort Ebey State Park.

From the parking lot near the campground gate, walk 0.1 mile on the Park Road, passing the WAIF (Whidbey Animals' Improvement Foundation) shelter, and come to the Kettles Trail's eastern trailhead. Now head west, first through a nice shady grove and then farmland upon crossing Jacobs Road. Then gradually descend, passing through another forest grove and more beautiful pasture lands. In spring and summer flowers line the way.

At 1.5 miles come to the Main Street traffic light. Cross the road and pass a pedestrian overpass spanning SR 20, which you can take if you want to divert to downtown Coupeville. Otherwise, continue west on the Kettles Trail. At 1.8 miles come to a trail junction just before reaching S Ebey Road.

Poppies along the Kettles Trail

Here a path heads 0.5 mile left to parallel S Ebey Road and SW Terry Road, terminating at Main Street.

The Kettles Trail continues northwest, traversing the wide expanse of Ebey's Prairie. Views across the prairie out toward the Olympics are divine. Pass a pumpkin patch and clusters of wildflowers in season. The way then begins to climb. Cross Sherman Road and climb some more—then steeply drop—and climb again, passing a cattle farm. At 2.8 miles come to the junction with the fairly new Kettles Spur Trail, which leads

0.75 mile to the Pratt Loop Trail. The Kettles Trail then skirts forest, coming to its paved ending at the Kettles Gate Trailhead at 3.6 miles.

GO FARTHER

If you want to run or walk the entire Kettles Trail, continue west on the unpaved trail through the Kettles Recreation Area. The path first follows an old road on a fairly level course, then enters Fort Ebey State Park and becomes single-track on hilly terrain. It crosses a park road (limited parking; Discover Pass required) before terminating in the park's campground in 1.7 miles. From here you can walk a short connector trail to the day-use parking area (Discover Pass required) near the gun battery if you plan to leave a vehicle at this end of the trail.

Rhododendron County Park near the trail's southern terminus contains several wonderful trails for hiking and running. The trails traverse mature forest with an understory of—no surprise here—rhododendrons. The entire 192-acre park is fairly flat, making its trails perfect for all ages. The old Rhodie Road (now a trail) goes 0.75 mile through the heart of the park, connecting the campground to the playfields and day-use parking area. From the campground gate parking area, take Grandpa's Legacy to the Rhodie Road to the Boundary Trail to the Campground Trail for a 2.2-mile grand loop of the park.

35 Joseph Whidbey State Park

DISTANCE:	2 miles of trails
ELEVATION GAIN:	Up to 80 feet
HIGH POINT:	80 feet
DIFFICULTY:	Easy
FITNESS:	Walkers, hikers
FAMILY-FRIENDLY:	Yes

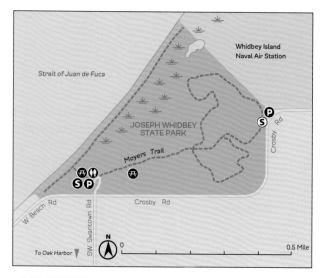

DOG-FRIENDLY:	On leash
AMENITIES:	Privies, water, picnic tables
CONTACT/MAPS:	Washington State Parks
GPS:	N 48° 18.484', W 122° 42.850'
BEFORE YOU GO:	Discover Pass required.

GETTING THERE

Driving: From Oak Harbor follow State Route 20 to SW Swantown Avenue (turnoff is 0.6 mile southwest of S Oak Harbor Street and Pioneer Way junction). Now continue on SW Swantown Road for 2.9 miles to its end at a junction with W Beach and Crosby roads. Continue straight into Joseph Whidbey State Park to the trailhead. The main park entrance (and facilities) are closed from October 1 to April 1. During this period, park at alternative trailheads on W Beach Road and Crosby Road.

Not as well-known as Whidbey Island's other very popular state parks, Joseph Whidbey State Park contains a delightful little trail system and a quiet stretch of beach: quiet in terms

A tunnel of greenery along the Moyers Trail

of crowds, but not decibels, as the park borders the Whidbey
Island Naval Air Station—so expect to periodically hear some
maneuvering jets. The views toward the San Juan Islands,
however, should hold most of your attention.

GET MOVING

From the small parking area a path heads left about 0.1 mile
directly to the beach: the direction most folks head. During
low tide, the park beach is a good one to walk. It has some nice
sandy stretches, but like most Salish Sea beaches, it has rocky
sections, too. There is a trail, however, that runs the full length
of the beach, ending in 0.6 mile at the air station boundary.
Do heed any posted warnings about closures, active firings,
and maneuvers if you are contemplating going beyond the
park boundary.

   For a longer hike follow the Moyers Trail north from the
main parking lot. The wide trail takes off through a verdant
deciduous jungle. The forest is mostly mature alder with some
grand firs thrown in here and there. Head-high stinging nettles

lining the path deserve your attention, unless you enjoy being zapped. The way passes an old rock pool of some sort—a reminder that this park was once part of a homestead.

At 0.3 mile come to a junction at a large, rolling meadow. Here you can make a 1.2-mile loop by following the main trail either direction through the meadow and adjacent woodlands. There are a handful of secondary paths that divert from the loop and may lead you astray, but they usually just loop back to the main trail. Throughout the spring and summer savor the blossoms of the Nootka roses lining the way. In winter, portions of the trail can get downright soggy and the small sections that are planked (you'll soon find out) are inadequate for keeping your feet from getting muddy.

The loop brushes up along a small wetland pond that usually provides some good bird-watching. The trail also passes through an alternative trailhead on Crosby Road—the starting point for when the main lot is closed.

36 Oak Harbor Waterfront Trails

DISTANCE:	More than 3 miles of trails
ELEVATION GAIN:	Up to 50 feet
HIGH POINT:	50 feet
DIFFICULTY:	Easy
FITNESS:	Walkers, runners
FAMILY-FRIENDLY:	Yes, and jogging stroller- and wheelchair-friendly
DOG-FRIENDLY:	On leash
AMENITIES:	Restrooms, water, picnic tables, benches, interpretive signs, playfields, playgrounds, campground
CONTACT/MAPS:	Oak Harbor Parks and Recreation and Naval Air Station Whidbey Island; no maps online
GPS:	N 48° 17.021', W 122° 37.923'
BEFORE YOU GO:	Park closed from 10:00 PM to 5:00 AM; stay on trail on naval property.

Maylor Point Trail

GETTING THERE

Driving to Maylor Point Trailhead: From the junction of S Oak Harbor Street and Pioneer Way on State Route 20, continue east on SE Pioneer Way for 0.3 mile. Turn right onto SE City Beach Street, following arterial (SE Bayshore Drive to Midway Boulevard) for 0.5 mile to traffic light. Then turn right on SE Pioneer Way and drive 0.4 mile, bearing right onto Maui Avenue. After 0.2 mile turn right onto SE Catalina Drive and continue 0.1 mile to trailhead parking at the city marina.

Driving to Windjammer Park Trailhead: From the S Oak Harbor Street and Pioneer Way junction on SR 20, continue east on SE Pioneer Way for 0.3 mile. Turn right onto SE City Beach Street and follow for 0.1 mile to park and trailhead.

Driving to Freund Marsh Trailhead: From the S Oak Harbor Street and Pioneer Way junction on SR 20, continue west on W Pioneer Way for 0.5 mile. Then turn left onto SW Scenic

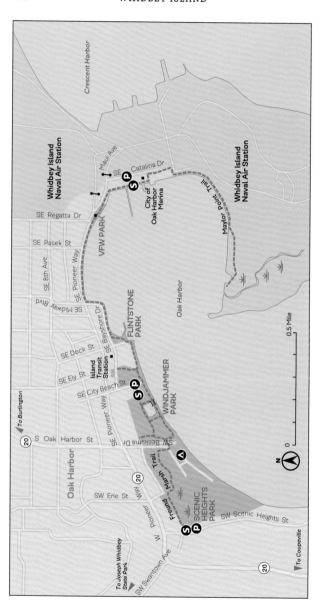

Crescent Harbor

Whidbey Island Naval Air Station

Maui Ave

SE Catalina Dr

City of Oak Harbor Marina

Maylor Point Trail

Whidbey Island Naval Air Station

SE Regatta Dr

SE Pasek St

VFW PARK

SE 8th Ave

SE Pioneer Way

SE Midway Blvd

SE Bayshore Dr

FLINTSTONE PARK

SE Dock St

Oak Harbor

Island Transit Station

SE Ely St

SE City Beach St

WINDJAMMER PARK

SE Pioneer Way

S Oak Harbor St

SW Beeksma Dr

20

To Burlington

Oak Harbor

W Pioneer Way

SW Erie St

20

Freund Marsh Trail

SCENIC HEIGHTS PARK

SW Scenic Heights St

0.5 Mile

N

0

To Joseph Whidbey State Park

SW Swantown Ave

20

To Coupeville

Heights Street and proceed 0.1 mile to trailhead and parking on your left.

Transit: Island Transit Routes 1NB, 1SB 3, 6, 10, 12, and 411W

Take to one, two, or all three of Oak Harbor's waterfront trails and experience one, two, or three different aspects of Whidbey Island's largest city's thriving and beautiful harbor. Walk or run through a marsh teeming with birds, a beach swarming with folks of all persuasions, and a pretty peninsula providing excellent wildlife habitat and wonderful views of the city. With the help of some sidewalks, all three of the trails are threaded together, allowing you to do them all in one go.

GET MOVING

The trails at Maylor Point, Freund Marsh, and Windjammer Park all make excellent walks or runs alone, but consider combining them for a much longer and satisfying workout. A one-way walk or run from the Freund Marsh Trailhead to trail's end on Maylor Point is 2.9 miles, so you're looking at 5.8 miles out and back. Add a small side loop in Windjammer Park to your route and you can easily get a 10K (6.2 miles) run or walk.

For Maylor Point, locate the trailhead at the far southern end of the marina. Here it enters the Whidbey Island Naval Air Station, which has generously granted an easement for the public to use this trail. Note, however, that the trail can be closed at any time. Keep your dog leashed and stay on the trail.

After passing a few station buildings and crossing a road, the trail resumes as a wide gravel path. The way is perfectly level, hugging the harbor shoreline. To the east a dense forest of fir stands. To the west it's Nootka rose bushes, salt flats, sun-bleached beached logs, and open water. It's quite pretty and feels far removed from the city, which is visible across the harbor. At 0.8 mile the trail ends at a point west on the peninsula of Maylor Point.

From the marina you can follow good sidewalk and paths west along the harbor toward Windjammer Park. The route climbs a small bluff, providing good views, and you'll pass some Garry oaks, the only native oak tree in Washington—it pushes its northern limits here on Whidbey and the nearby San Juan and Gulf islands. Development has significantly reduced the oak groves in and around this city named after them.

Pass through the VFW Park and by the Island Transit Station. About 1 mile from the marina veer left off of the path paralleling SE Bayshore Drive and explore small Flintstone Park: kids will like the Flintstone mobile there, while Boomers will wax nostalgic. The path continues along the shore, passing some residences and utilizing a boardwalk before emerging at Windjammer Park about 1.2 miles from the marina.

Here a paved path continues along the shore. Other paved paths branch off it and traverse around the busy city park. Walk or run by good beaches and over a small bridge spanning a lagoon outlet. At 1.6 miles from the marina, pass the park's campground and cross SW Beeksma Drive. Then turn right and follow a path, soon reaching the eastern trailhead for the Freund Marsh Trail.

Follow this wonderful trail through the old Freund homestead (named for one of the first non-Native settlers on Whidbey Island), since transformed into a natural area. Birdlife is prolific here, as are deer. The trail passes across open grassy areas and through thickets of dense shrubs. There are a couple of bridges spanning old channels. Take time to read and appreciate the colorful interpretive signs. At 2.1 miles reach the trail's western trailhead at Scenic Heights Park. Here is a good overlook of the marsh as well as a kiosk with interesting historical background of the area.

37 **Dugualla State Park**

DISTANCE:	More than 5 miles of trails
ELEVATION GAIN:	Up to 500 feet
HIGH POINT:	440 feet
DIFFICULTY:	Easy to moderate
FITNESS:	Hikers, runners
FAMILY-FRIENDLY:	Yes
DOG-FRIENDLY:	On leash
AMENITIES:	None
CONTACT/MAPS:	Washington State Parks
GPS:	N 48˚ 20.393', W 122˚ 34.427'
BEFORE YOU GO:	Discover Pass required.

GETTING THERE

Driving from Oak Harbor: Follow State Route 20 east for 4 miles and turn right onto E Sleeper Road. Continue for 2.5 miles to road's end and trailhead.

Driving from Burlington: Follow SR 20 west for 24 miles and turn left onto E Sleeper Road. Continue for 2.5 miles to road's end and trailhead.

Beach on Skagit Bay

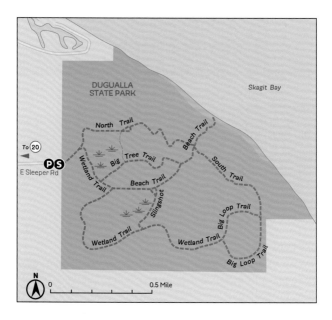

A former Department of Natural Resources property once slated to be logged, Dugualla is now a 586-acre satellite of Deception Pass State Park. Hike or run more than 5 miles of trails here, following old skid roads and newer single-tracks through mature stands of timber, including a couple of old-growth giants. There is also a mile of coastline to walk when the tide is low. And while this property lacks amenities other than trail signs, it also lacks crowds.

GET MOVING

The trees are tall and many are quite old at Dugualla State Park. It was all slated to be clear-cut until a deal was made to move this impressive stand of timber to state park protection in 1992. Years passed after the transfer, and the property remained undeveloped and undiscovered. In the past few years, volunteers with organizations like the Washington Trails Association and Switmo have helped develop and mark an excellent network of trails in the park. But the crowds have yet to arrive. One Labor Day, my family and I had the entire park to ourselves.

The trailhead is pretty unimpressive, marked by an old gate and nothing else. Perhaps someday, Washington State Parks will at least build a parking lot and privy. Head past the gate on an old logging road, now called the North Trail. In 0.1 mile you'll reach a junction. If you're intent on making a beeline to the beach, the shortest route is about a mile either straight via the North Trail to the Beach Trail or right via the Wetland Trail to the Beach Trail. In either case, after a small climb you will descend steeply to the beach. You will also pass the Big Tree junction graced—by no surprise here—a big tree: in this case a giant old-growth Douglas fir.

There are actually many old and large trees—western hemlocks and grand firs in addition to the Douglas firs in Dugualla. You can find them along the North Trail and Big Tree Trail, which also makes for a fairly direct but hillier approach to the beach. The beach can be explored at low tide, but be prepared for some muck. Enjoy good views across Skagit Bay to Goat and Ika islands in the Skagit Wildlife Area. Goat Island was the site of Fort Whitman, one of the Puget Sound coastal fort installations of the last century and the least known and visited of the old forts.

If you're looking to put some mileage in at Dugualla, a grand circuit of the park via the North, South, Big Loop, and Wetlands trails will yield 3.1 miles. Add a trip to the beach to that loop and you're up to 3.6 miles. Add some connector trails and you can easily hike or run more than 5 miles here.

38 Deception Pass State Park: Goose Rock and Cranberry Lake

DISTANCE:	More than 7 miles of trails
ELEVATION GAIN:	Up to 800 feet
HIGH POINT:	484 feet
DIFFICULTY:	Easy to moderate
FITNESS:	Walkers, hikers, runners
FAMILY-FRIENDLY:	Yes
DOG-FRIENDLY:	On leash
AMENITIES:	Water, restrooms, campground, picnic tables and shelters, interpretive displays
CONTACT/MAPS:	Washington State Parks/Green Trails, Deception Pass/Anacortes Community Forest Lands No. 41S
GPS:	N 48° 24.203', W 122° 38.848'
BEFORE YOU GO:	Discover Pass required.

GETTING THERE

Driving from Oak Harbor: Follow State Route 20 north for 9.4 miles to a traffic light. Turn left here into Deception Pass State Park. Proceed past park entrance station and in 0.4 mile turn left at a junction (signed for West Beach). Continue another 0.7 mile to a large parking area and trailhead.

Driving from Burlington: From exit 230 on I-5, head west on SR 20 for about 18.5 miles, crossing the Deception Pass Bridge and coming to a traffic light. Turn right here into Deception Pass State Park. Proceed past the park entrance station and in 0.4 mile turn left at a junction (signed for West Beach). Continue another 0.7 mile to a large parking area and trailhead.

Transit: Island Transit Route 411W

One of the highest points on Whidbey Island, Goose Rock offers the closest thing to "mountain climbing" on the island.

Hiker enjoying the view from Goose Rock

Though not exactly a lofty summit, the views are spectacular and far-reaching. From Goose's open, grassy slopes and mossy, rocky ledges, bask in sunshine while catching a gaggle of surrounding peaks and islands. Cranberry Lake is a tasty little destination too. And in between these two landmarks lies a beautiful ancient forest.

GET MOVING

With over three million annual visitors, Deception Pass is Washington's most popular state park. Created during the Great Depression, great elation is what you'll feel after taking to this park's trails—more than 40 miles of them traverse the 4134-acre park. Many were developed in the 1930s by the Civilian Conservation Corps (CCC). The park consists of large tracts of land on both sides of Deception Pass—the strait separating Whidbey Island from Fidalgo Island.

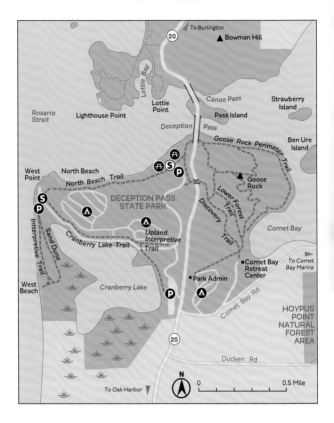

For a short, easy, and level hike, follow Sand Dune Interpretive Trail south toward West Beach. This 1.2-mile trail provides views of both placid Cranberry Lake and the vast Salish
Sea. You can access the shore here and walk more than 1.5
miles of mostly sandy and cobble beach. You can also follow
the 1-mile Cranberry Lake Trail west from the parking lot. It
first parallels the road you came in on, providing access to
the campground and offering some good views of Cranberry
Lake. It then crosses the road and travels along Cranberry's

Trail above Cornet Bay

eastern shoreline. The 0.2-mile Upland Interpretive Trail splits off from the Cranberry Lake Trail, offering more to explore.

More ambitious hiking can be done by following the North Beach Trail east from West Beach. This trail provides access to the beautiful and walkable North Beach and follows a wooded bluff above it. At 0.9 mile it reaches the North Beach parking area (alternative start for Goose Rock).

For Goose Rock continue east and reach a junction with the Discovery Trail at 0.2 mile. Continue east, climbing about 100 feet to the Deception Pass Bridge. Built in 1935 as a Public Works Administration (PWA) project, the attractive 976-foot steel cantilever bridge, along with its sister 511-foot steel arched Canoe Pass Bridge, is one of the most photographed structures in the state. Marvel at them and gaze down below at the turbulent waters funneling though Deception Pass.

Admire too, the view out to Deception Island and the rugged headlands comprising the pass.

Now hike under the bridge and come to a junction. The trail right is the Northwest Goose Rock Summit Trail (part of the Pacific Northwest Trail), which heads 0.4 mile to the summit. Take it for a direct route or head left on the Goose Rock Perimeter Trail and other ascending options. The perimeter trail passes excellent viewpoints of Deception Pass as well as Strawberry and Ben Ure islands. The latter was named for a notorious human trafficker.

At 0.3 mile from the bridge a trail heads right, climbing 0.3 mile to meet up with the Northwest Goose Rock Summit Trail 0.2 mile from the summit. The perimeter trail soon continues left at water's edge. It then climbs about 150 feet up a grassy madrona-lined ledge above sparkling Cornet Bay and then loses all that elevation, dropping back to sea level.

At 1.2 miles from the bridge reach another junction. Here the Goose Rock Summit Trail heads right, climbing 450 feet in 0.4 mile to the summit. Take it and return on the Northwest Goose Rock Summit Trail, or continue left, soon coming to another junction. Here the Lower Forest Trail heads right 0.6 mile to the Northwest Goose Rock Summit Trail. The better option is to continue left another 0.1 mile to another junction.

The way left goes to the Cornet Bay Retreat Center. The way right—the Discovery Trail—travels 0.7 mile through beautiful old-growth forest. It then ducks under SR 20 through a CCC-built underpass and comes to the North Beach parking area.

You have a lot of options for hiking up and over and around Goose Rock. Whichever way you decide, be sure to take the 0.1-mile trail on the summit to a series of open ledges granting excellent views. Look north to Mount Erie; west to the Strait of Juan de Fuca, the Olympic Mountains, and the San Juan Islands; and south to Mount Rainier rising above a rolling Whidbey Island countryside. Watch fighters take off from the nearby naval air base. You're sure to hear them!

39

Deception Pass State Park: Hoypus Point Natural Forest Area

DISTANCE:	More than 9 miles of trails
ELEVATION GAIN:	Up to 600 feet
HIGH POINT:	400 feet
DIFFICULTY:	Easy to moderate
FITNESS:	Walkers, hikers, runners, cyclists
FAMILY-FRIENDLY:	Yes
DOG-FRIENDLY:	On leash
AMENITIES:	Water, restrooms, marina, and picnic tables
CONTACT/MAPS:	Washington State Parks/ Green Trails, Deception Pass/Anacortes Community Forest Lands No. 41S
GPS:	N 48° 24.117', W 122° 37.295'
BEFORE YOU GO:	Discover Pass required.

GETTING THERE

Driving from Oak Harbor: Follow State Route 20 north for 9.4 miles to a traffic light. Turn right here onto Cornet Bay Road. Then continue 1.4 miles to parking and trailhead at Cornet Bay Marina.

Driving from Burlington: From exit 230 on I-5, head west on SR 20 for about 18.5 miles, crossing the Deception Pass Bridge and coming to a traffic light. Turn left here onto Cornet Bay Road. Then continue 1.4 miles to parking and trailhead at Cornet Bay Marina.

Escape from the Deception Pass State Park masses at this quiet corner of the sprawling park. Amble on miles of interconnecting trails amid ancient conifers on a tract of Whidbey Island that has withstood the pressures of the modern world. Admire towering firs that witnessed Captain George Vancouver's 1789 sailing, when he mistakenly took the island for a

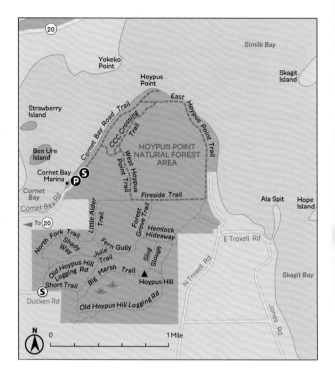

peninsula. Realizing his error, Vancouver bestowed the name Deception upon the strait that had fooled him for a river.

GET MOVING

The Hoypus Point Natural Forest Area consists of a large undeveloped parcel on Hoypus Point and Hoypus Hill. Much of the northern portion of this area contains big old-growth Douglas firs and ancient western red cedars. These trees are among the largest and oldest on the island and surely would have been logged if Washington State Parks hadn't acquired this tract from the Department of Natural Resources back in 1992. Managed now as a natural forest area, these trees will continue to defy the ages and amaze their admirers.

Hiker admiring towering old-growth at Hoypus Point

   To start exploring this area, head east on the gated eastern stretch of Cornet Bay Road (now closed to motor vehicles). In 0.3 mile come to a junction with the West Hoypus Point Trail. It heads south, immediately climbing and connecting to other trails in the natural area. You can continue walking east on the road another 0.4 mile to reach the East Hoypus Point Trail. This trail also heads south and climbs, connecting to other trails.

Cornet Bay Road continues east for another 0.25 mile, terminating at an old ferry crossing. Here take in a splendid view of Similk Bay, Skagit Island, Mount Erie, and Mount Baker. When tides are low you can explore the beach below.

If you're looking for a short loop in the natural area, retreat 0.25 mile to the East Hoypus Point Trail and take it. After a short climb reach a junction with the CCC Crossing Trail, a possible return route. Continue straight on the East Hoypus Point Trail, a pleasant way through towering old trees. Climb again and in 1 mile brush up against the backyards of a few residences as the trail follows the park boundary. Catch glimpses of Ala Spit and Hope Island out in Skagit Bay. At 1.4 miles the way makes a sharp right turn, now following the Fireside Trail. After a short, steep climb the trail crosses a 380-foot saddle on Hoypus Hill. It then drops steeply on a sometimes muddy and slick way. Pass the Forest Grove Trail to the left, and at 2 miles arrive at a junction with the West Hoypus Point Trail.

Turn right on a level grade through lush bottomlands, coming to a trail junction at 2.4 miles. You can head left, returning back to your start at 3 miles. The trail passes a massive Douglas fir en route. Or, you can continue right 0.4 mile on the CCC Crossing Trail. Then head left 0.2 mile on the East Hoypus Point Trail back to Cornet Bay Road for a 3-mile loop followed by a 0.7-mile return on the road to your start.

Much of the southern half of the natural area consists of younger forest. A good network of trails and old logging roads (converted to trails) crisscrosses it. An alternative trailhead for this area can be reached from Ducken Road. This area sees some mountain bike and equestrian use but is generally lightly traveled. If you're interested in doing a grand run or hike around the natural area's periphery, count on clicking off 7.5 miles. You can easily double that distance by including several loops to take in the trails you missed. And if after exploring this area you're wondering what a Hoypus is, you're not alone. Named by famed explorer Charles Wilkes in 1841, he left no explanation of what it means. Come to your own conclusion.

Next page: *Young hiker enjoying a deserted Cama Beach*

CAMANO ISLAND

Camano Island and Whidbey Island make up Island County. But the smaller, much less populated Camano Island (about 15,000 residents) has more in common with nearby Stanwood and northwestern Snohomish County than it does with Whidbey, mainly due to access. To quote a famous New England expression—*you can't get there from here*. There are no bridges or ferries connecting the two islands, requiring lengthy trips via the mainland to get from one island to the other—unless of course you have your own boat.

Connected to the mainland by a bridge on State Route 532, Camano is easily accessible from Everett and the Skagit Valley. Lacking incorporated communities and with very few commercial enterprises, many Camano Islanders work on the mainland. Many folks who call Camano home are also retirees, adding to the island's laid-back atmosphere. Until fairly recently there were very few places to hike on the island. But a new, large state park and several new preserves laced with trails have changed that. The Whidbey Camano Land Trust has been active on this island, too, securing important parcels for conservation along with building and expanding the island's trail system.

40 Iverson Spit Preserve

DISTANCE:	1.2 miles of trails
ELEVATION GAIN:	Minimal
HIGH POINT:	20 feet
DIFFICULTY:	Easy
FITNESS:	Walkers, hikers
FAMILY-FRIENDLY:	Yes
DOG-FRIENDLY:	On leash
AMENITIES:	Privy, picnic tables
CONTACT/MAPS:	Island County Parks. No map online but available in pamphlet *Walking the Camano Island Trails* (donation; see Friends of Camano Island Parks website for pamphlet outlets).
GPS:	N 48° 12.664', W 122° 26.531'

GETTING THERE

Driving: From Everett follow I-5 north to exit 212. Then head west on State Route 532 for 10 miles (passing through Stanwood) to Camano Island. At the traffic light, take a left onto N Sunrise Boulevard and drive 2.5 miles. Then turn left onto E Iverson Beach Road and continue 0.5 mile. Next bear left onto Iverson Road and continue 0.5 mile to trailhead at road's end.

A 120-acre park on a small spit jutting into Livingston Bay at the northern reaches of Port Susan, Iverson Spit provides a lot of scenery—but not much walking. Only a little more than a mile of trail graces this quiet park. But the bird-watching is excellent and so are the views of the Cascades across the bay. When the tide is out, there's good beach walking to be had on a sandy shoreline. So, despite the short length of its trails, you'll probably end up spending some time in this lovely park.

Mount Baker rises above Livingston Bay

GET MOVING

From the trailhead you can head directly to a pair of observation decks favored by area birders. Iverson Spit is a great spot to watch for wintering snow geese and other waterfowl.

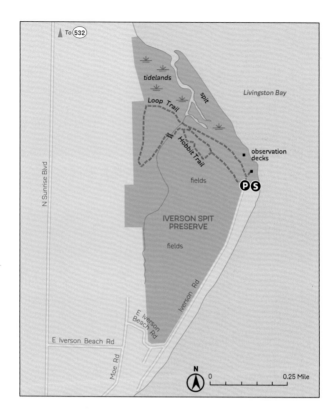

The area also occasionally serves as a temporary home for snowy owls. If you're not interested in birds—or there just aren't many around—cast your eyes outward instead to a wonderful view across Port Susan. Enjoy excellent viewing of prominent Three Fingers Mountain, popular Mount Pilchuck, and breathtaking Mount Baker. The view is especially stunning in winter when the peaks are shrouded in snow.

If the tide is low, consider heading out for a walk on the small sandy spit. However, you'll need to first negotiate a row of big old-growth driftwood logs, which litter the spit like an old logging boom. If you're ready for some walking on terra firma instead, follow the Loop Trail west. Note that much of the preserve occupies former salt flats reclaimed by levees built by farmers in the first half of the twentieth century. The trails here can get wet and muddy during the rainy season.

The 1-mile Loop Trail heads west out on a levee lined with madronas and head-high rosebushes and blackberry brambles. Views are good north into a salt marsh where herons and ducks are prolific. You'll pass a shortcut trail and an old dike channel before reaching the end of the levee. The trail heads south through forest and wetlands along the base of a steep bluff, then circles back, heading along the edge of a field and small drainage channel. It makes a bridged crossing of the channel before meeting back up with the shortcut trail. From here it returns to the parking lot via an old farm road.

Extend your walk by taking the short but enchanting Hobbit Trail, which branches off from the Loop Trail near the shortcut junction and meets back up with the Loop Trail after about 0.2 mile. Kids will love this trail, which utilizes boardwalks while wiggling through a tunnel of stunted and gnarled hawthorns.

GO FARTHER

Check out nearby Barnum Point County Park (access from N Sunrise Boulevard), which opened in the summer of 2018. The Whidbey Camano Land Trust, with the help of numerous generous donors (including $10,000 from Stanwood High School students), helped expand this once-small park to 129 acres. The trust then developed 2.5 miles of hiking trails through the preserve. The park also contains 1 mile of beach to explore. It was the last large undeveloped, unprotected piece of shoreline remaining on the island—a spectacular property that now belongs to the public to forever cherish and enjoy.

41 Camano Ridge Forest Preserve

DISTANCE:	More than 5 miles of trails
ELEVATION GAIN:	Up to 450 feet
HIGH POINT:	560 feet
DIFFICULTY:	Easy to moderate
FITNESS:	Hikers, runners
FAMILY-FRIENDLY:	Yes
DOG-FRIENDLY:	On leash
AMENITIES:	None
CONTACT/MAPS:	Island County Parks. No map online but available in pamphlet *Walking the Camano Island Trails* (donation; see Friends of Camano Island Parks website for pamphlet outlets).
GPS:	N 48° 12.763', W 122° 30.378'
BEFORE YOU GO:	Preserve is open to hunting—wear orange in season.

GETTING THERE

Driving: From Everett follow I-5 north to exit 212. Then head west on State Route 532 for 10 miles (passing through Stanwood) to Camano Island. At the traffic light continue straight on NE Camano Drive. After 1 mile turn right onto E Cross Island Road. Continue for 1.9 miles and turn left onto N Camano Ridge Road. Then drive 0.9 mile to the parking area and trailhead on your left.

One of the largest undeveloped tracts of land remaining on the island, this former Department of Natural Resources property is a great place for long, contemplative forest walks. While some of this 400-plus-acre preserve was logged a few decades ago, much of it contains stands of stately mature timber. Seasonal wetlands grace the broad ridge, adding bird and insect song in the spring and summer to these dark and usually quiet woods.

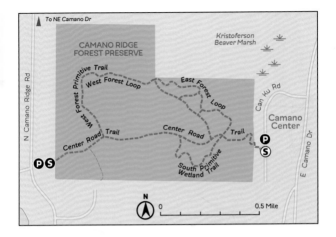

GET MOVING

Of all of Camano Island's hiking areas, the Camano Ridge Forest Preserve is the least developed. There are no amenities here—including no trail signs (be sure to bring a map)—but the Friends of Camano Island Parks hope to rectify that soon. The biggest improvement of late is the new parking lot at the western trailhead, which was opened in 2018. The eastern trailhead (located 0.4 mile up Can Ku Road off of E Camano Drive) still lacks a parking lot (park on road shoulder) and signage. Don't let the lack of trail signs discourage you, however, as the trail system here is pretty straightforward.

The preserve sits on a long, broad ridge, very near the island's high point (which is located on adjacent private property). If you start your hike or run (these trails make excellent running routes) from the west, you can do a series of loops without much elevation gain. If you start from the eastern trailhead, however, you'll get a good hill workout of about 250 feet to start. Starting from either end and hiking the periphery will yield 3 to 3.5 miles.

Center Road Trail

From the western trailhead follow an old logging road known as the Center Road Trail, passing a gate. Then gently ascend and after about 0.4 mile come to a junction with the West Forest Loop (read on for more on this). The Center Road, lined with alders, continues east, gently descending. In about 0.2 mile the South Primitive Wetland Trail branches off of it to the right. This trail skirts wetlands and traverses groves of large trees, returning to the Center Road Trail.

The Center Road Trail continues east, soon coming to a junction with the East Forest Loop Trail. If you continue on the

Center Road Trail, you'll come to another junction (about a mile from the west trailhead). Here, heading left, is the other end of the East Forest Loop. This 1.5-mile or so loop utilizes single-track and old road and traverses attractive forest on a mostly gentle sloping ridge. The trail (old road) to the right eventually becomes single-track and it descends and winds about 0.4 mile to the eastern trailhead.

Two lesser-used trails form shortcuts on the East Forest Loop if you are short on time or energy. There is also a pretty decent trail—the West Forest Primitive Trail—that branches off of the East Forest Loop where it bends back east. This trail eventually becomes an old road and returns to the Center Road Trail near the western trailhead. This trail, when combined with the southern leg of the East Forest Loop, forms the West Forest Loop—a slightly shorter loop than the East Forest Loop. Confused? Just take your map with you and enjoy your hike or run, and hopefully by the next time you check this place out there will be some signage in place!

42 Four Springs Lake Preserve

DISTANCE:	1.5 miles of trails
ELEVATION GAIN:	Up to 200 feet
HIGH POINT:	400 feet
DIFFICULTY:	Easy
FITNESS:	Hikers
FAMILY-FRIENDLY:	Yes
DOG-FRIENDLY:	On leash
AMENITIES:	Privy, picnic tables
CONTACT/MAPS:	Island County Parks. No map online but available in pamphlet *Walking the Camano Island Trails* (donation; see Friends of Camano Island Parks website for pamphlet outlets).
GPS:	N 48° 11.416', W 122° 30.827'

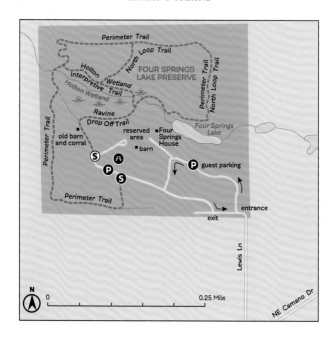

GETTING THERE

Driving: From Everett follow I-5 north to exit 212. Then head west on State Route 532 for 10 miles (passing through Stanwood) to Camano Island. At the traffic light continue straight on NE Camano Drive, and after 2.6 miles bear right onto N Camano Hill Road. Continue 2.4 miles and turn right onto Lewis Lane. Then drive 0.2 mile, entering Four Springs Lake Preserve and parking for trailheads.

A former farm and homestead, the Four Springs Lake Preserve contains a lot of charms and surprises. One surprise is the lake—it's more like a tiny pond, but it is spring-fed. The preserve's other charms include an old barn, vintage farm equipment, weathered fence posts, wetlands, mature forest,

Hiker negotiating a wet section of the Holton Wetland Interpretive Trail

and a small little ravine. There's a wonderful trail system at the 50-acre preserve, too.

GET MOVING

At the center of the preserve sits the Four Springs House overlooking the tiny Four Springs Lake. The house was occupied by the previous owners of this parcel before it was bought in 2001 for a park. Don't be surprised if you see a bunch of vehicles in the parking lot and well-dressed folks mulling around—the house is used for weddings and other functions throughout the year. The trails, however, are almost always pretty quiet.

You can start on the Perimeter Trail, which as its name suggests travels (mostly) around this squared parcel. This 1-mile trail passes through an old pasture and old orchard, crosses a small stream, goes up and down through mature second-growth forest, and passes by the Four Springs Lake. The trail ends in a ravine housing the lake and its outlet creek.

You can then hike back to your start via the 0.1-mile Ravine Drop Off Trail to an old barn and corral, from where it is another 0.1 mile back to the parking area. Do check out the barn and its old equipment. If the 1.2-mile hike around the preserve wasn't enough, do some backtracking and add the short 0.2-mile Holton Wetland Interpretive Trail and 0.1-mile North Loop Trail to the mix. The trails can get a little slick during the rainy season, especially in the ravine. But the rains help keep the little creek flowing and the ravine wetlands lush.

43 Elger Bay Preserve

DISTANCE:	2.5 miles of trails
ELEVATION GAIN:	Up to 200 feet
HIGH POINT:	225 feet
DIFFICULTY:	Easy
FITNESS:	Hikers, runners
FAMILY-FRIENDLY:	Yes
DOG-FRIENDLY:	On leash
AMENITIES:	Interpretive signs
CONTACT/MAPS:	Island County Parks. No map online but available in pamphlet *Walking the Camano Island Trails* (donation; see Friends of Camano Island Parks website for pamphlet outlets).
GPS:	N 48° 08.75', W 122° 28.135'
BEFORE YOU GO:	Park at the school parking lot only during weekends and school vacations.

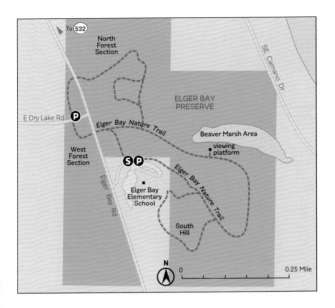

GETTING THERE

Driving: From Everett follow I-5 north to exit 212. Then head west on State Route 532 for 10 miles (passing through Stanwood) to Camano Island. At the traffic light continue straight on NE Camano Drive. Continue on this main arterial, which becomes E Camano Drive, for 5.8 miles. Then bear right onto Elger Bay Road and proceed for 1.4 miles. Next turn left into the Elger Bay Elementary School entrance and proceed a few hundred feet to the trailhead parking (marked with a kiosk) on your left. **Note:** If school is in session, park on the shoulder of E Dry Lake Road (junction 0.1 mile north of the school entrance on Elger Bay Road). You can access the loop trail here.

   Transit: Island Transit Route 2C

Author and son do a limbo under a tree limb

Enjoy **2.5 miles of quiet woodland trails** in this 150-plus-acre preserve located on a ridge north of Elger Bay. A former Washington Department of Natural Resources property, logging ceased here in the 1980s, with the land being transferred to the county for a new school and nature preserve. The preserve wraps around the school, allowing for an outdoor classroom—but students of all ages are welcome to roam the trails here. A few remnant large trees are scattered about and a large beaver marsh breaks up the monotony of the forest—and provides for some good wildlife observation.

GET MOVING

The trails here are well-maintained and the junctions well-marked. Thanks to the nearby school there are also some interpretive signs throughout the preserve. The Elger Bay Nature Trail is a 2.2-mile grand circuit of the preserve. It pieces together old woods roads and newer sections of trail. The loop can be shortened by taking several shortcuts along the way—or it can be lengthened by taking these shortcuts to create a series of loops within the loop.

Head north from the trailhead and immediately come to a junction for the loop. Either left or right will work. If you do the loop clockwise, continue north. At 0.1 mile come to a junction. The loop continues left, but it involves crossing busy Elger Bay Road twice. If you prefer to skip that section, head right instead, soon connecting back to the loop.

If you go left, carefully cross Elger Bay Road. The trail then turns north, crossing E Dry Lake Road (parking access when school is in session) and traverses a scrappy section of forest infested with invasive holly. The way then turns east to once again cross Elger Bay Road. The trail then follows an old road through a uniform stand of stately Douglas firs. Go right at a junction—unless you want to shorten the loop. Go right at the next junction, pass a big grand fir, and at 0.9 mile come to another junction—this one with the shortcut trail allowing a bypass of the road crossings.

The loop continues left, coming to a platform overlook of the large beaver marsh at 1 mile. Scan the bulrushes for ducks, herons, and beavers. The interpretive panel here is riddled with bad spelling and grammar. Perhaps the writers weren't paying enough attention at the nearby school! The loop continues on an old road through a forest logged in the 1980s. It then bends back westward and comes to a junction at 1.5 miles. The way left is the loop continuation. It travels 0.4 mile up and over South Hill and is a nice rolling section of trail through mature forest. It passes an outdoor amphitheater before descending the hill. You can bypass it if you'd like by heading straight at this junction and returning to the loop in 0.1 mile. Otherwise go left, and it will be 0.3 mile back to the trailhead.

44 Cama Beach Historical State Park

DISTANCE:	More than 5 miles of trails
ELEVATION GAIN:	Up to 400 feet
HIGH POINT:	340 feet
DIFFICULTY:	Easy to moderate
FITNESS:	Walkers, hikers, runners
FAMILY-FRIENDLY:	Yes
DOG-FRIENDLY:	On leash
AMENITIES:	Restrooms, water, picnic tables, interpretive displays, overnight cabins, camp store, café
CONTACT/MAPS:	Washington State Parks
GPS:	N 48˚ 08.528', W 122˚ 30.753'
BEFORE YOU GO:	Discover Pass required.

GETTING THERE

Driving: From Everett follow I-5 north to exit 212. Then head west on State Route 532 for 10 miles (passing through Stanwood) to Camano Island. At the traffic light continue straight on NE Camano Drive. After 2.6 miles bear right onto N Camano Hill Road. Continue 3.3 miles and turn left onto W Camano Drive. Then drive 2.8 miles, turning right into Cama Beach State Park. Proceed 0.3 mile to parking and trailheads.

Most visitors to this **486-acre state park** on Saratoga Passage come to stay at one of the restored 1930s cabins or play at the park's nearly 1 mile of beach. The popular park, however, is laced with excellent trails that often see very little activity. Hike or run to a secluded little lake, up a ridge bounding with

A young hiker heads down the Beach Trail.

blackberries, through groves of mature conifers, and atop a coastal bluff granting excellent maritime views.

GET MOVING

One of Washington's newer and most alluring state parks, Cama Beach protects one of the last remaining intact fishing resorts on Puget Sound. In operation from 1934 to 1989, Cama Beach became a state park in the 1990s. The structures have since been renovated to retain their 1930s charm. The cabins are available for overnight stays and have been a big hit since the parks department began operating them. Reservations are required and often must be made well in advance. Consider staying, with a hike and run right from your cabin.

From the large parking area, several trails branch out. You can easily spend all day exploring them. The wide and lit-at-night Beach Trail descends west 125 feet or so to the cabins. Walk among them and check out the Center for Wooden Boats. When the tide is low, walk out on the nearly 1-mile-long

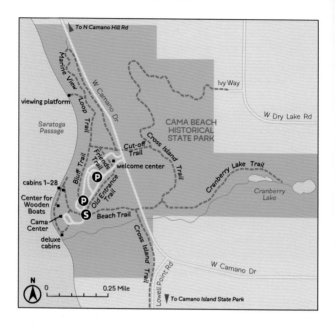

beach. The northern reaches are particularly attractive, beneath bluffs of draping madronas. From the parking area the Beach Trail also travels east, utilizing an old road through a grove of towering maples and grand firs. In 0.3 mile it comes to a junction just before crossing W Camano Drive.

Here you can head right on the Cross Island Trail. This 1-mile stretch of trail leaves the park and parallels Lowell Point Road, eventually entering Camano Island State Park (see Trail 45) and connecting to that park's fine trails. You can also carefully cross W Camano Drive and in 0.1 mile come to another junction—this one with the Cranberry Lake Trail. The Cross Island Trail continues left here through thick forest. In 0.3 mile the Cut-off Trail leads left to cross the road, returning to the main part of the park and connecting to the Marine View Loop Trail. The Cross Island Trail continues another 0.9 mile, bending east and following an old roadway. It climbs about 150 feet, traversing thick forest graced with salal and native Northwest blackberry bushes (not that invasive Himalayan species). It ends on W Dry Lake Road where, if you are inclined, you can walk right about 1.4 miles to the Elger Bay Preserve (see Trail 43).

The Cranberry Lake Trail is a particularly delightful path. Take it through alders and snowberry bushes and across boardwalks, gently climbing a small ridge. At 0.7 mile reach Cranberry Lake, a shallow marshy wetland surrounded by cattails, spirea, and huckleberry bushes. In springtime, it's a good spot for bird-watching.

From the main parking area you can also head out on the Old Entrance Trail, Friends Trail, and Bluff Trail. The three trails make a nice 0.7-mile loop around the parking areas and welcome center. From the Bluff Trail you can also head north on the park's newest trail, the Marine View Loop Trail. This 1-mile loop traverses attractive forest along the 170-foot or so coastal bluff north of the cabins. A trail branches from it connecting to a neighborhood on the park's northern boundary. There are a series of informational platforms along the way, which are worth a stop. And there is a spur trail leading to a platform with an excellent view of the cabins along the beach below, a true highlight of this trail and park.

45 Camano Island State Park

DISTANCE:	More than 4 miles of trails
ELEVATION GAIN:	Up to 300 feet
HIGH POINT:	300 feet
DIFFICULTY:	Easy to moderate
FITNESS:	Walkers, hikers, runners
FAMILY-FRIENDLY:	Yes
DOG-FRIENDLY:	On leash

West Bluff section of the Loop Trai

AMENITIES:	Restrooms, water, picnic tables and shelters, interpretive displays, campground and cabins
CONTACT/MAPS:	Washington State Parks
GPS:	N 48° 07.318', W 122° 29.461'
BEFORE YOU GO:	Discover Pass required.

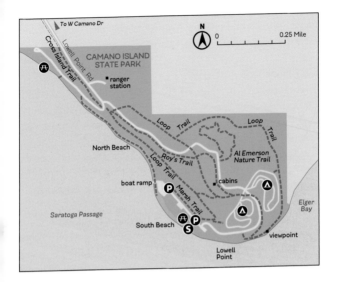

GETTING THERE

Driving: From Everett follow I-5 north to exit 212. Then head west on State Route 532 for 10 miles (passing through Stanwood) to Camano Island. At the traffic light continue straight on NE Camano Drive. After 2.6 miles bear right onto N Camano Hill Road. Continue 3.3 miles and turn left onto W Camano Drive. Then drive 3.2 miles (passing through Cama Beach State Park) and turn right onto Lowell Point Road. Now follow this road 0.8 mile into Camano Island State Park. Bear left and follow main park road (passing camping area) for 1.1 miles to its end at a large day-use parking area and trailhead.

Located on Lowell Point on Saratoga Passage, Camano Island State Park offers excellent woodland strolls and beach wanderings on its 244 acres. Climb steps through ravines for good heart conditioning and stroll manicured trails through stands of blotchy-barked madronas and stately firs atop coastal bluffs. From its beach and bluff tops, Camano Island

State Park offers dramatic glimpses of the lofty Cascade and Olympic peaks hovering over sparkling waters.

GET MOVING

There are several miles of trails within this park and you can create both short and long loops. The park has pieced together a handful of the trails as the Loop Trail. It's 2.6 miles, includes a lot of the park's best attributes, and makes for a perfect introduction to the park—or a wonderful route to return and do over again. To do this loop, locate the southern trailhead for the Marsh Trail on the east side of the parking lot.

If you want to hike this short trail first, head left on it. It parallels the large parking area, terminating at the northern trailhead on the west side of the parking lot. Along the way look for eagles perched on tall firs. For the loop, head right, up an attractive ravine shaded by mature maples and cloaked with waxy salal and boughs of ferns. Immediately come to a junction. Turn left. With the aid of steps, steeply but briefly climb out of the ravine and come to another junction. Here the loop trail goes either left or right. Head right to finish with the pretty West Bluff section (although you can go left if you prefer).

Soon come to another junction. Bear right and continue climbing, coming to the group camp area. Go right through the cabin camp area and then pick up the trail once more. Pass the amphitheater, weave through the campground, cross the main park road, and then parallel it south for a short distance, eventually heading back into the woods.

Now get ready to enjoy spectacular Puget Sound scenery. The trail turns left, hugging the rim of a 150-foot bluff rising above Elger Bay. Stop at numerous viewpoints to marvel straight down Saratoga Passage's gleaming waters. Scope out Mount Rainier, Mount Pilchuck, Baring Mountain, and others on the eastern horizon.

Continue along the bluff, soaking up scenery and sea breezes. The trail eventually turns inward, coming to another junction. Head right in thick forest along the park's periphery. Reach a 300-foot high point before beginning a slow descent, dipping in and out of small ravines along the way. Pass some giant old-growth Douglas firs before coming to another junction. The trail left returns to the campground. Head right, dropping steeply. Cross the park road, pass Roy's Trail on the left (an alternative return) and the Cama Beach Connector Trail (Cross Island Trail) on your right, then follow the Loop Trail left back to your beginning along more high bluffs. Pause frequently to take in captivating views across the sound of the jagged Olympic Mountain peaks rising above Whidbey Island's chalky bluffs and emerald forests. Then come to a familiar junction and head back down the ravine to your start.

Of course, there is more to explore aside from the Loop Trail. You can follow a trail along the shoreline from the North Beach to the South Beach—or when the tide is low, walk the beach. For a good leg-stretcher, follow the Cross Island Trail 1 mile to Cama Beach Historical State Park (see Trail 44), where you can continue walking on that park's extensive trail system. Or, for a short, mellow loop, check out the Al Emerson Nature Trail.

Rolling lawn at Jennings Memorial Park (Trail 22)

ACKNOWLEDGMENTS

RESEARCHING AND WRITING *Urban Trails: Everett* was fun, gratifying, and a lot of hard work. I couldn't have finished this project without the help and support of the following people. A huge thank-you to all the great people at Mountaineers Books, especially publisher, Helen Cherullo; editor-in-chief, Kate Rogers; and project manager, Melissa Kiepke.

A big thank-you to my copyeditor, Sarah Gorecki, for her attention to detail and thoughtful suggestions, which helped make this book a finer volume. I also want to thank my wife, Heather, and son, Giovanni, for accompanying me on many of the trails in this book. A big thanks, too, to Judith and Richard Romano, Suzanne Gerber, Susan Elderkin, Virginia Scott, Delfina McKoy, Megan McGrew, Lynne Jordan, and Dennis Clark for providing me with excellent trail company. And thanks so much to Jessica Larson, Land Steward for the Whidbey Camano Land Trust, for your invaluable help. And I thank God for watching over me and keeping me safe and healthy while I hiked and ran all over Everett and its environs!

Spencer Island estuary and Mount Pilchuck (Trail 14)

RESOURCES

CONTACTS

City Parks

Al Borlin Park
(360) 863-4557
www.monroewa.gov/Facilities/Facility/Details/Al-Borlin-Park-2

Arlington Airport Trail
(360) 403-3470
www.arlingtonwa.gov/index.aspx?page=259

Big Gulch
(425) 263-8180
http://archive.ci.mukilteo.wa.us/Page.asp?NavID=157

Forest Park
(425) 257-8300 ext. 2
https://everettwa.gov/Facilities/Facility/Details
/Forest-Park-23

Japanese Gulch Conservation Area
(425) 263-8180
http://archive.ci.mukilteo.wa.us/Page.asp?NavID=321

Jennings Memorial Park
(360) 363-8400
http://marysvillewa.gov/Facilities/Facility/Details/16

Lake Tye Park
(360) 863-4557
www.monroewa.gov/Facilities/Facility/Details/Lake-Tye-Park-8

Langus Riverfront Park
(425) 257-8300 ext. 2
https://everettwa.gov/Facilities/Facility/Details
/Langus-Riverfront-Park-27

Lowell Riverfront Park
(425) 257-8300 ext. 2
https://everettwa.gov/Facilities/Facility/Details
/Lowell-Riverfront-Park-30

North Creek Trail
(425) 921-5736
www.cityofmillcreek.com/facilities/facility/details
/North-Creek-Trail-19

Osprey Park
(360) 793-2231
https://ci.sultan.wa.us/osprey-park

Scriber Lake Park
(425) 670-5000
www.lynnwoodwa.gov/PlayLynnwood/Parks/Scriber-Lake
-Park.htm

Terrace Creek Park (Candy Cane Park)
(425) 776-9173
www.cityofmlt.com/Facilities/Facility/Details
/Terrace-Creek-Park-Candy-Cane-Park-9

Windjammer Park (Oak Harbor Waterfront Trails)
(360) 279-4756
www.oakharbor.org/page.cfm?pageId=192

Port of Coupeville

Greenbank Farm

(360) 222-3151

www.portofcoupeville.org/greenbank-farm.html

map: www.islandcountywa.gov/PublicWorks/Parks
/Documents/GreenbankFarm.pdf

Port of Everett

Everett Waterfront Trail

(425) 388-0602

www.portofeverett.com/recreation/waterfront-trails

Jetty Island

(425) 388-0602

www.portofeverett.com/recreation/beaches-kiteboarding
/jetty-island-290

Island County Parks

Camano Ridge Forest Preserve

(360) 679?-7335

www.islandcountywa.gov/PublicWorks/Parks/Pages/camano
-ridge.aspx

Double Bluff

(360) 679-7335

www.islandcountywa.gov/PublicWorks/Parks/Pages/double
-bluff.aspx

Elger Bay Preserve

(360) 679-7335

www.islandcountywa.gov/PublicWorks/Parks/Pages/elger
-bay.aspx

Four Springs Lake Preserve
(360) 679-7335
www.islandcountywa.gov/PublicWorks/Parks/Pages/four
-springs-house.aspx

Iverson Spit Preserve
(360) 679-7335
www.islandcountywa.gov/PublicWorks/Parks/Pages/iverson
-preserve.aspx

Kettles Trails
(360) 679-7335
www.islandcountywa.gov/PublicWorks/Parks/Pages/kettles
-trails.aspx

Rhododendron County Park
(360) 679-7335
www.islandcountywa.gov/PublicWorks/Parks/Pages
/rhododendron-park.aspx

Saratoga Woods, Putney Woods, and Metcalf Trust Trails
(360) 679-7335
www.islandcountywa.gov/PublicWorks/Parks/Pages/putney
-woods.aspx

National Park Service
Ebey's Landing National Historical Reserve
(360) 678-6084
www.nps.gov/ebla/index.htm

Snohomish County Parks
Centennial Trail
(425) 388-6600
https://snohomishcountywa.gov/Facilities/Facility/Details
/Centennial-Trail-33

Interurban Trail
(425) 388-6600
https://snohomishcountywa.gov/Facilities/Facility/Details
/Interurban-Trail-69

Lord Hill Regional Park
(425) 388-6600
https://snohomishcountywa.gov/Facilities/Facility/Details
/Lord-Hill-Regional-Park-35

Meadowdale Beach Park
(425) 388-6600
https://snohomishcountywa.gov/Facilities/Facility/Details
/Meadowdale-Beach-Park-56

Narbeck Wetland Sanctuary
(425) 388-5125
www.painefield.com/148/Narbeck-Wetland-Sanctuary

North Creek Park
(425) 388-6608
https://snohomishcountywa.gov/Facilities/Facility/Details
/North-Creek-Park-and-Water-Retention-Fac-103

Paradise Valley Conservation Area
(425) 388-6600
https://snohomishcountywa.gov/Facilities/Facility/Details
/Paradise-Valley-Conservation-Area-PVCA-66

River Meadows Park
(360) 435-3441
https://snohomishcountywa.gov/Facilities/Facility/Details
/River-Meadows-Park-46

Spencer Island
(360) 568-2482
https://snohomishcountywa.gov/Facilities/Facility/Details
/Spencer-Island-76

Washington State Parks
Cama Beach Historical State Park
(360) 387-1550
http://parks.state.wa.us/483/Cama-Beach

Camano Island State Park
(360) 387-3031
http://parks.state.wa.us/484/Camano-Island

Deception Pass State Park
(360) 675-3767
http://parks.state.wa.us/497/Deception-Pass

Dugualla State Park
(360) 675-3767
www.deceptionpassfoundation.org/around-the-park
/dugualla-state-park

Fort Casey Historical State Park
(360) 678-4519
http://parks.state.wa.us/505/Fort-Casey

Fort Ebey State Park
(360) 678-4636
http://parks.state.wa.us/507/Fort-Ebey

Joseph Whidbey State Park
(360) 678-4519
http://parks.state.wa.us/526/Joseph-Whidbey

South Whidbey State Park
(360) 331-4559
http://parks.state.wa.us/585/South-Whidbey

Whidbey Camano Land Trust
Admiralty Inlet Preserve
(360) 222-3310
www.wclt.org/projects/admiralty-inlet-preserve

Trillium Community Forest
(360) 222-3310
www.wclt.org/projects/trillium-community-forest

TRAIL AND CONSERVATION ORGANIZATIONS

Deception Pass Park Foundation
www.deceptionpassfoundation.org

Forterra
http://forterra.org

Friends of Camano Island Parks
www.friendsofcamanoislandparks.org

Friends of Ebey's Landing National Historical Reserve
www.friendsofebeys.org

Friends of Lord Hill Park
http://friendsoflordhill.com

Friends of Meadowdale Beach Park
www.facebook.com/Friends-of-Meadowdale
-Beach-Park-166716363380641

Friends of Narbeck Wetlands
www.narbeck.org/index.html

Japanese Gulch Group
http://japanesegulch.org

The Mountaineers
www.mountaineers.org

The Mountaineers, Everett Branch
www.mountaineers.org/about/branches-committees
/everett-branch/about

The Nature Conservancy
www.nature.org

Pacific Northwest Trail
www.pnt.org

Switmo
www.switmo.org

Washington State Parks Foundation
http://wspf.org

Washington Trails Association
www.wta.org

Washington Wildlife and Recreation Coalition
www.wildliferecreation.org

Whidbey Camano Land Trust
www.wclt.org

RUNNING AND HIKING CLUBS AND ORGANIZED RUNS, HIKES, AND WALKS AROUND EVERETT

Arlington Runners Club
Small running club that holds a handful of community races on the Arlington Airport Trails or the Centennial Trail. www.arlingtonrunnersclub.org

Cupcake Runs
A series of runs ranging in distance from 5K to 50K on the Centennial Trail. Finishers receive a cupcake and other goodies. Races benefit various local charities. www.cupcakeruns.com/home.html

Deception Pass 25K and 50K
Tough and challenging ultramarathon on Deception Pass State Park's trail system. Organized by the respected Rainshadow Running event company. www.rainshadowrunning.com/deception-pass-50k.html

Evergreen Trail Runs
Trail running race series that includes an event at Lord Hill. www.evergreentrailruns.com

Hike It Baby
National organization with chapters in Snohomish and Island counties focusing on group hikes with infants and toddlers. https://hikeitbaby.com

Jingle Trail 5K Fun Run and Walk
Family-friendly cross-country run held at Camp Casey and Fort Casey State Park. http://coupevillechamber.com/event/jingle-trail-5k-fun-run -and-walk

The Mountaineers

Seattle-based outdoors club that has an Everett branch involved in local conservation issues and coordinates group outdoor activities.
www.mountaineers.org

Northwest Trail Runs

Well-run series of trail runs that includes races at Paradise Valley Conservation Area and Fort Ebey's Kettles Trails.
http://nwtrailruns.com/events

Outdoor Afro Seattle

A community that reconnects African Americans with natural spaces and one another through a wide array of recreational activities, including hiking.
www.meetup.com/Outdoor-Afro-Seattle

Race the Reserve

Annual 5K, 10K, half marathon, and marathon held within Ebey's Landing National Historical Reserve.
http://racethereserve.com

Run26

Running specialty store in Mill Creek that supports local runners and running events. The store also sponsors group runs and events on the nearby North Creek Trail.
http://run26.net

Snohomish Running Company

Race event organization that puts on the Everett half marathon: course includes the Everett waterfront.
http://snohomishrunning.com/everett-half

Snohomish Women's Run
Women's-only half marathon race (and accompanying 10K) benefiting the Snohomish County Girls on the Run. Race partially held on the Lowell Riverfront Trail.
http://snohomishwomensrun.com

INDEX

ABOUT THE AUTHOR

Photo by Heather Romano

CRAIG ROMANO grew up in rural New Hampshire, where he fell in love with the natural world. He moved to Washington in 1989 and has since hiked more than 20,000 miles in the Evergreen state. An avid runner as well, Craig has run more than twenty-five marathons and ultra runs, including the Boston Marathon and the White River 50 Mile Endurance Run. Craig's mission is to run or hike every trail in Washington state, and every year he gets closer to his goal.

Craig is an award-winning author and co-author of twenty books; his *Columbia Highlands: Exploring Washington's Last Frontier* was recognized in 2010 by Washington secretary of state Sam Reed and state librarian Jan Walsh as a "Washington Reads" book for its contribution to Washington's cultural heritage. Craig also writes for numerous publications, tourism websites, and Hikeoftheweek.com.

When not hiking, running, and writing, he can be found napping with his wife, Heather, son, Giovanni, and cat, Giuseppe, at his home in Skagit County. Visit him at http://CraigRomano .com and on Facebook at Craig Romano Guidebook Author.

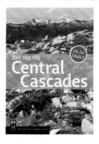
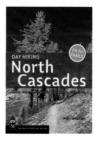